THE ART OF
ALFREDO CACCAMO

MINI-ARTBOOK - 2014

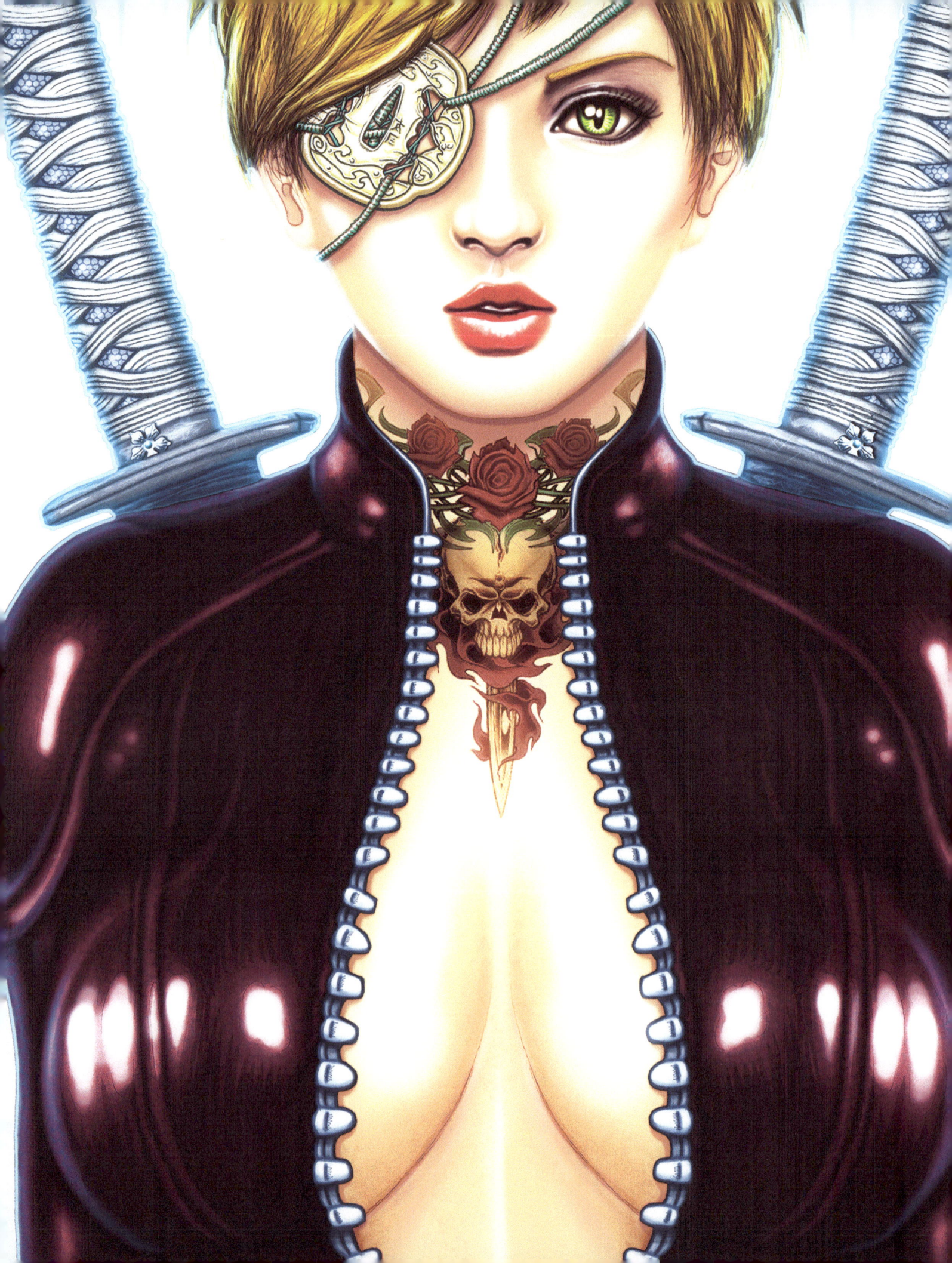

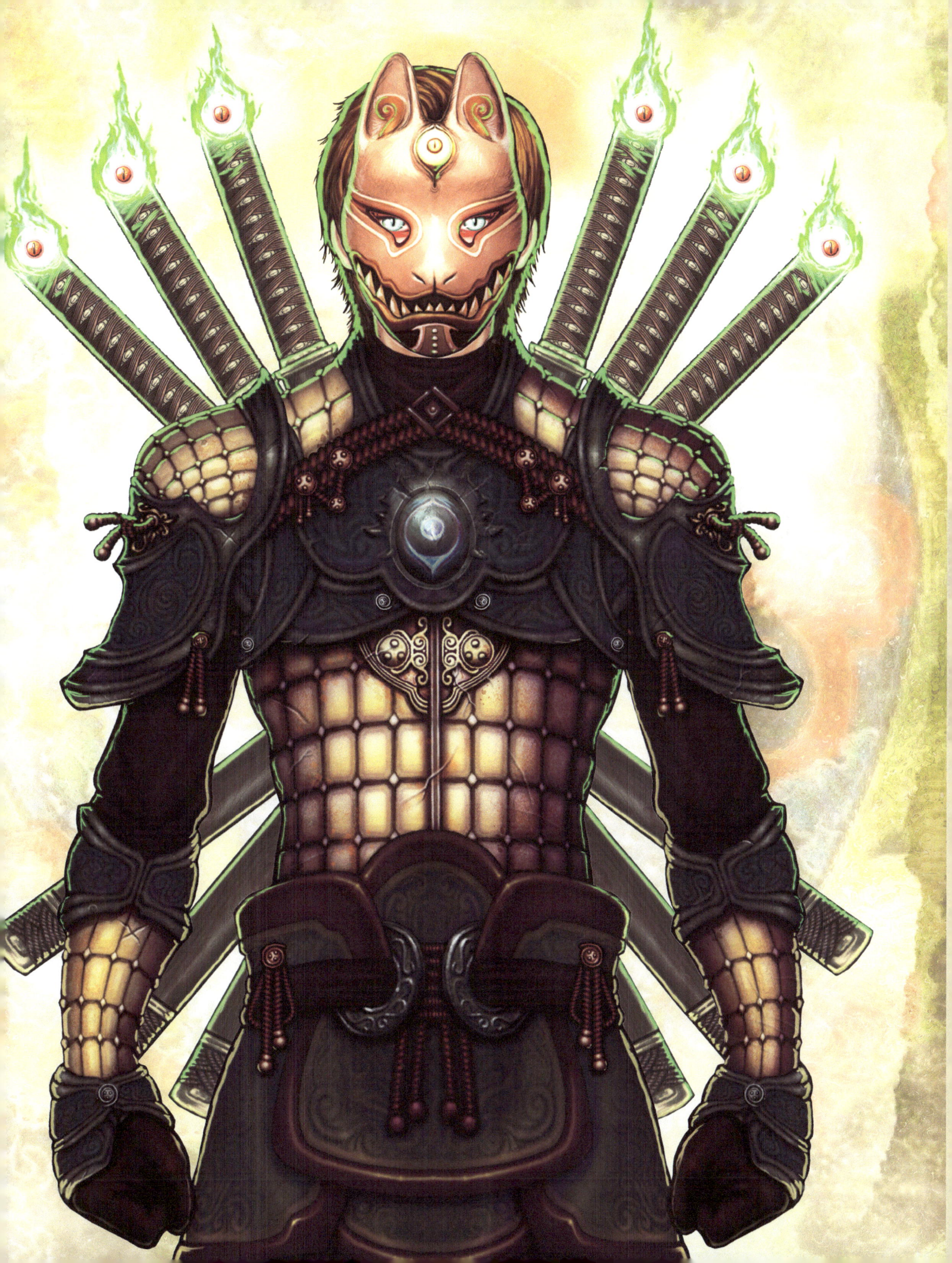

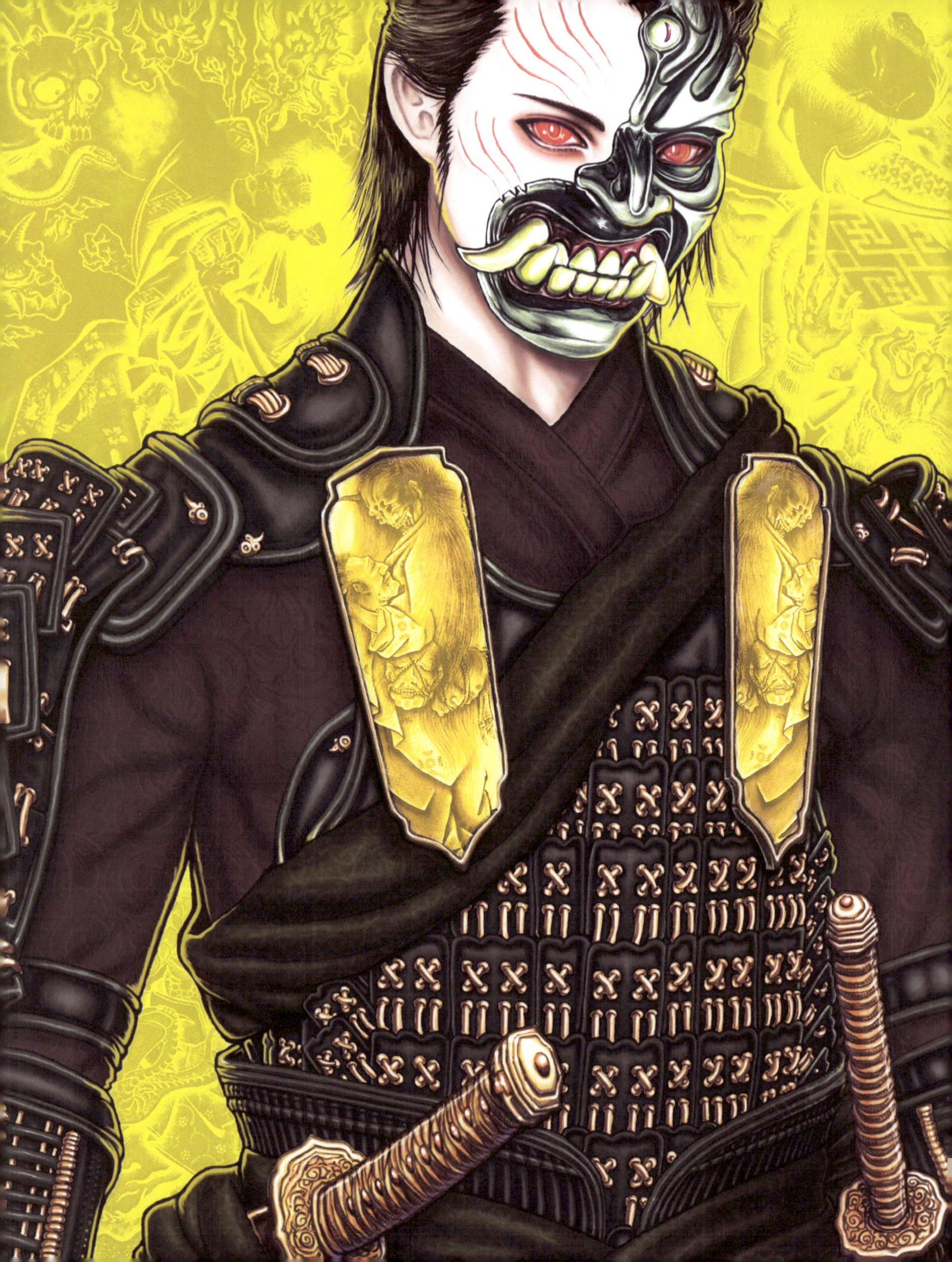

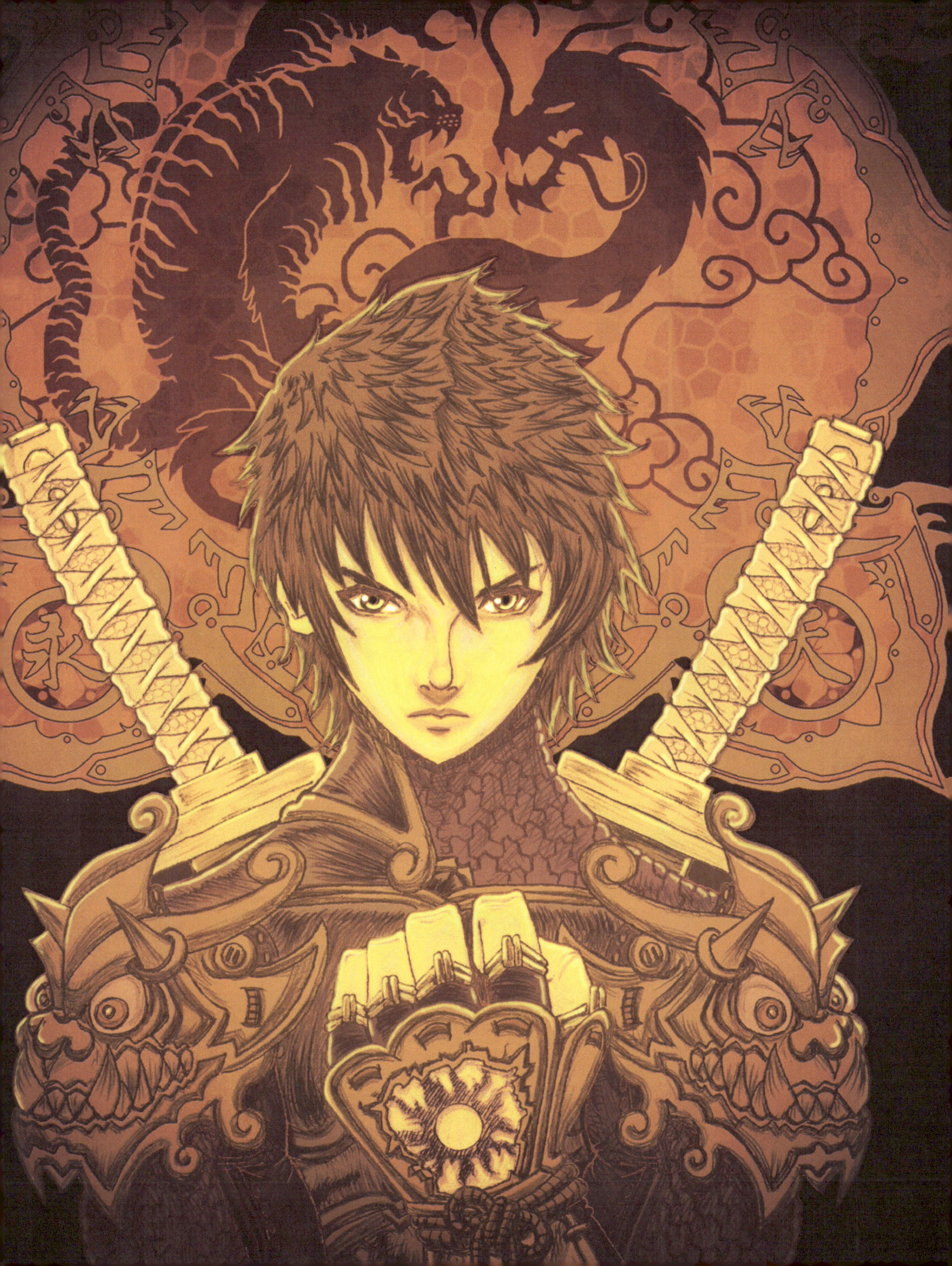

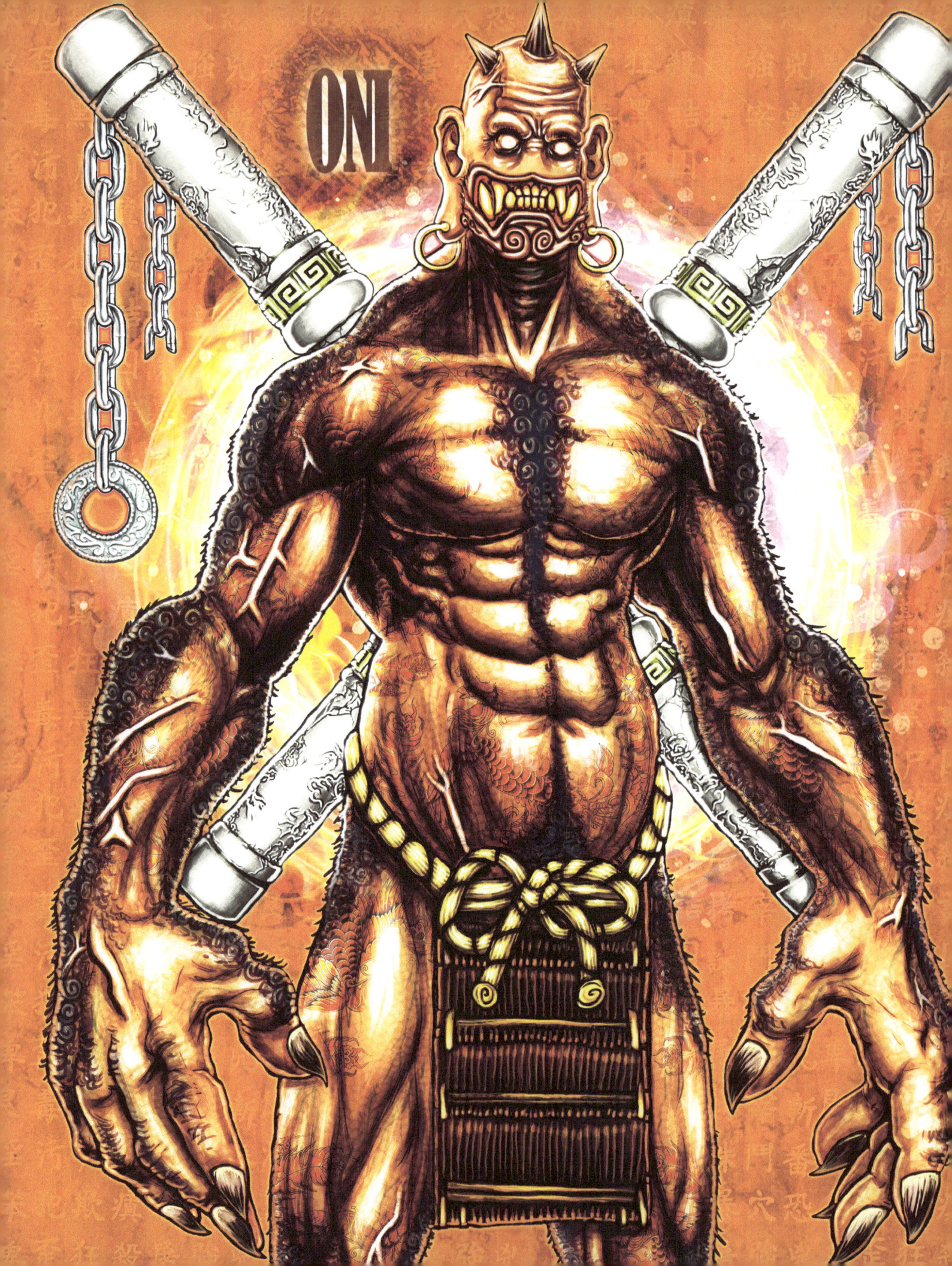

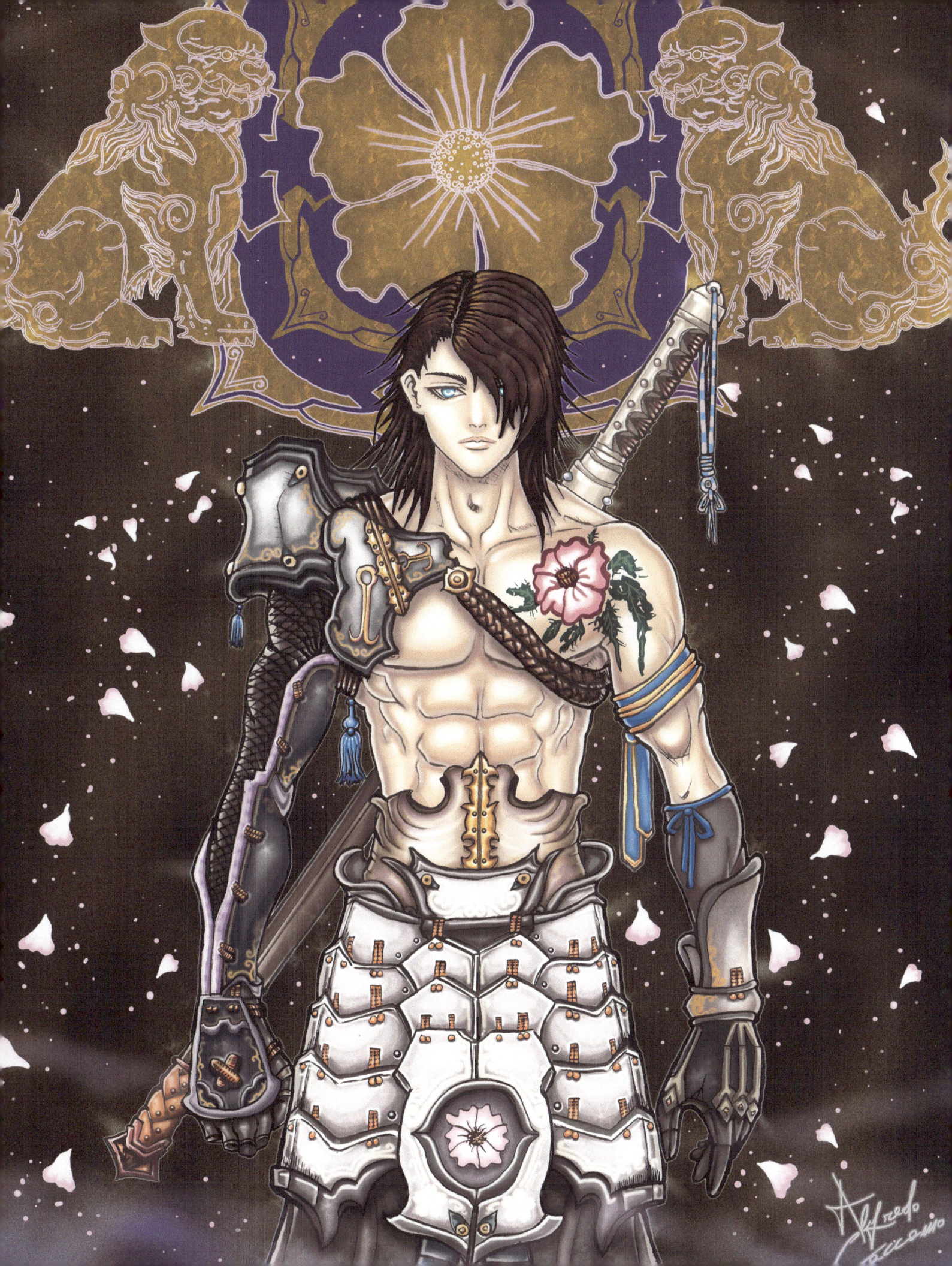

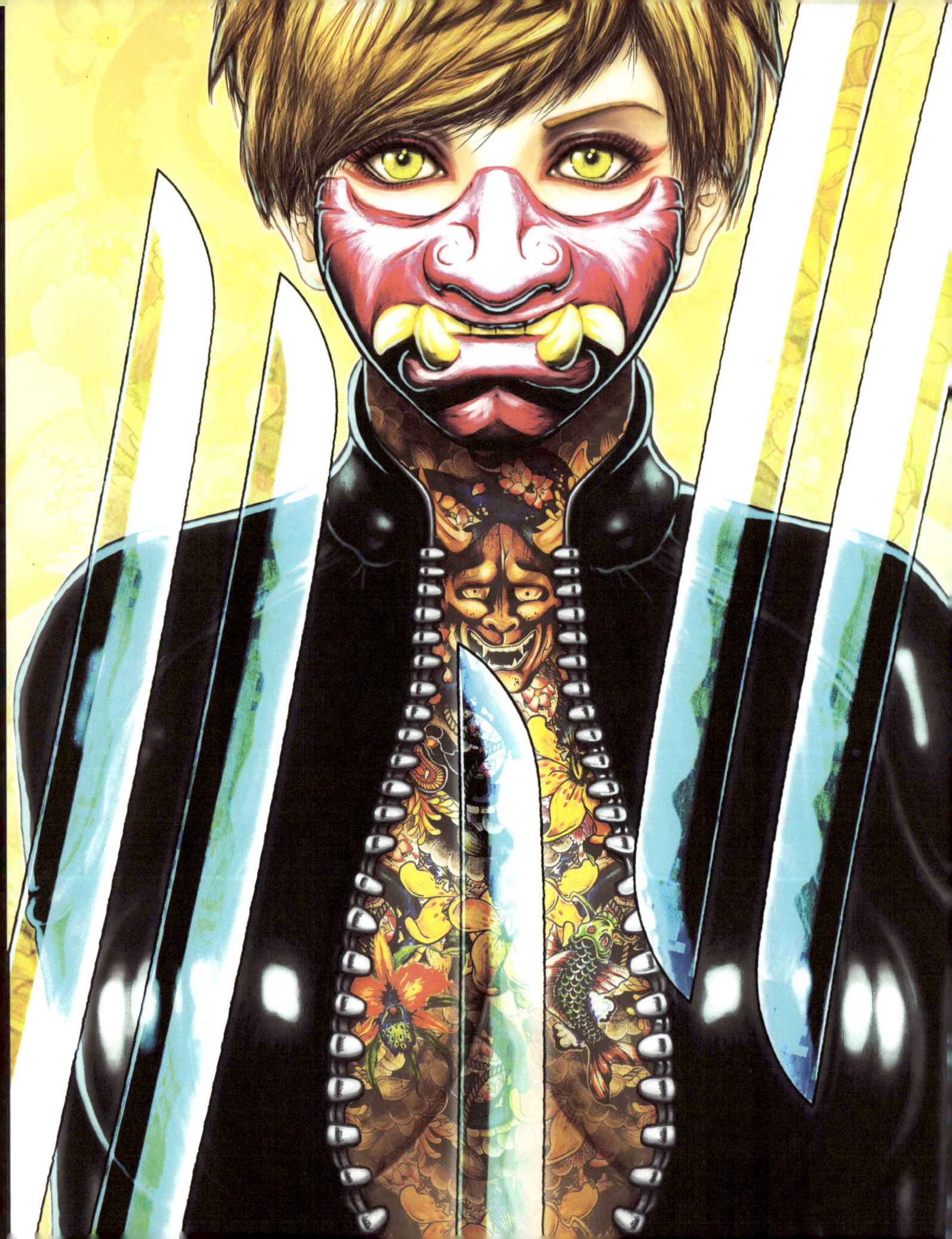

TUTORIAL ONI-MASK

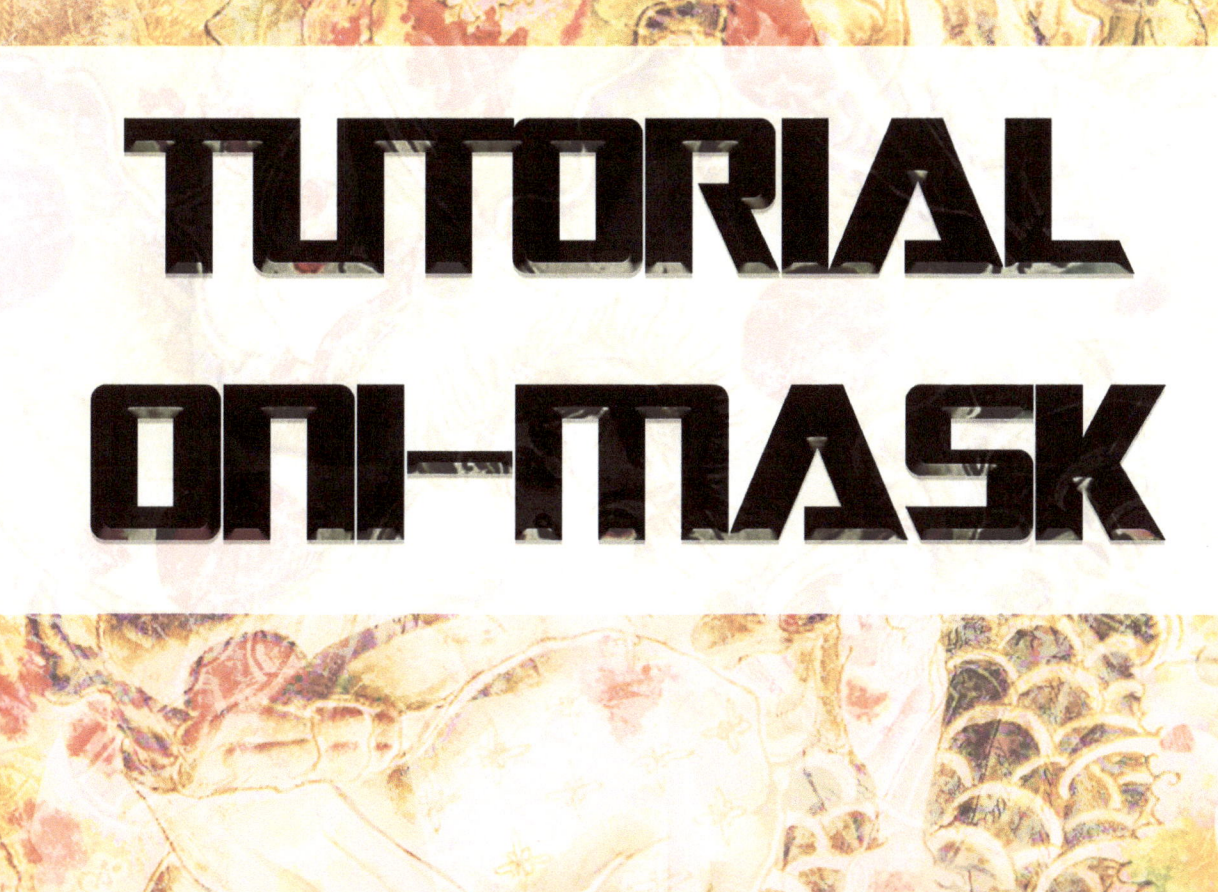

REFERENCES

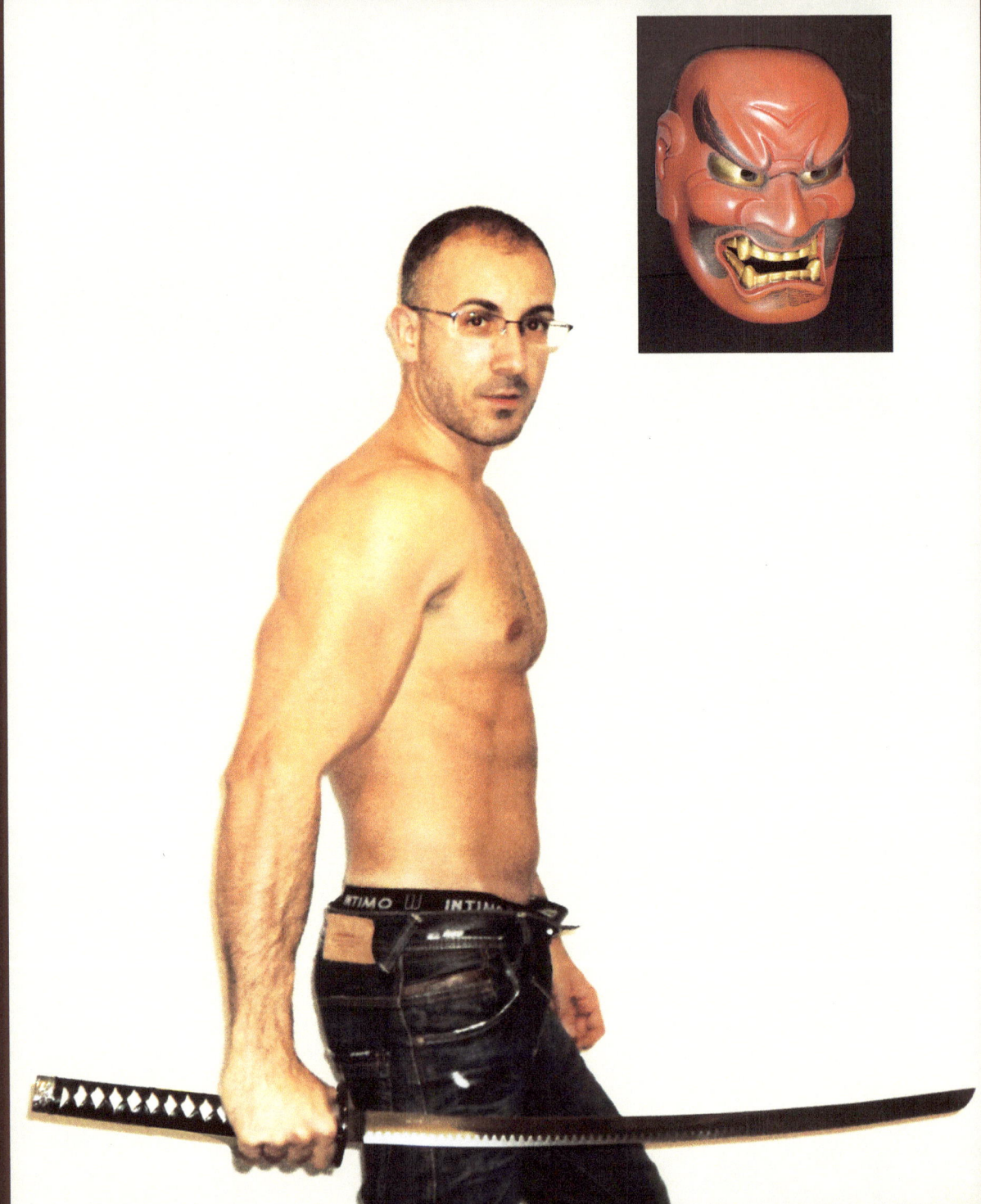

ME & MASK (PHOTOS)

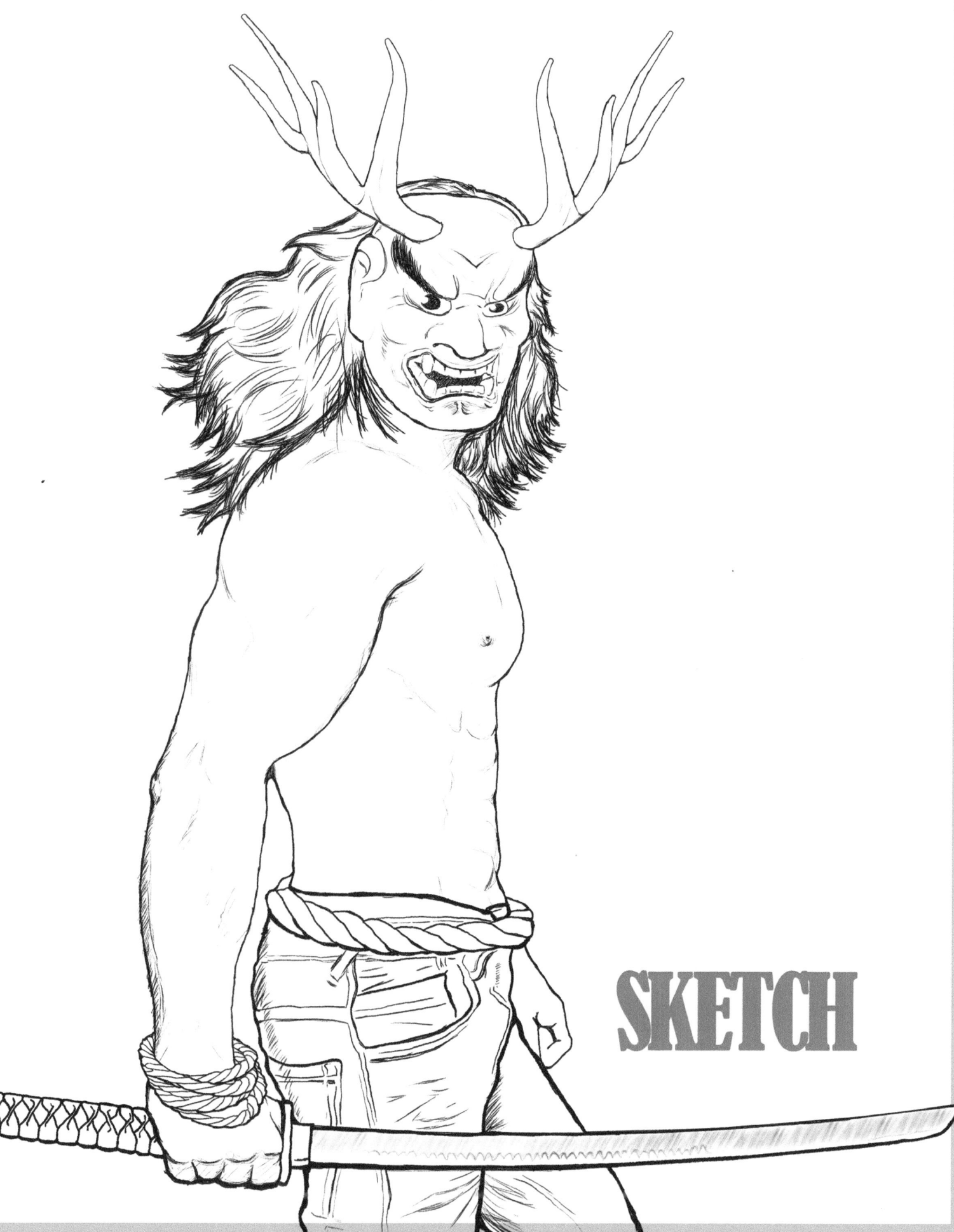

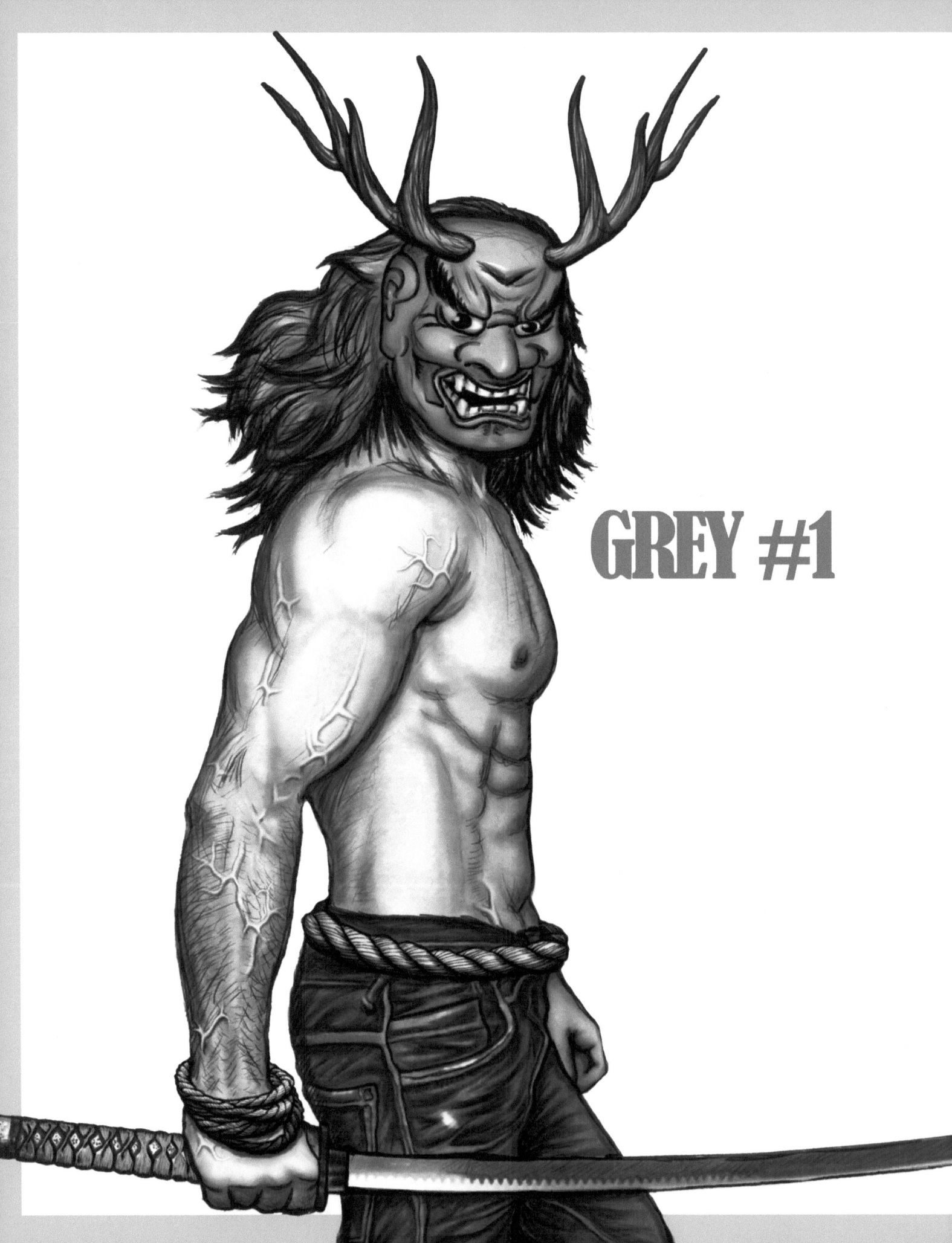

GREY #1

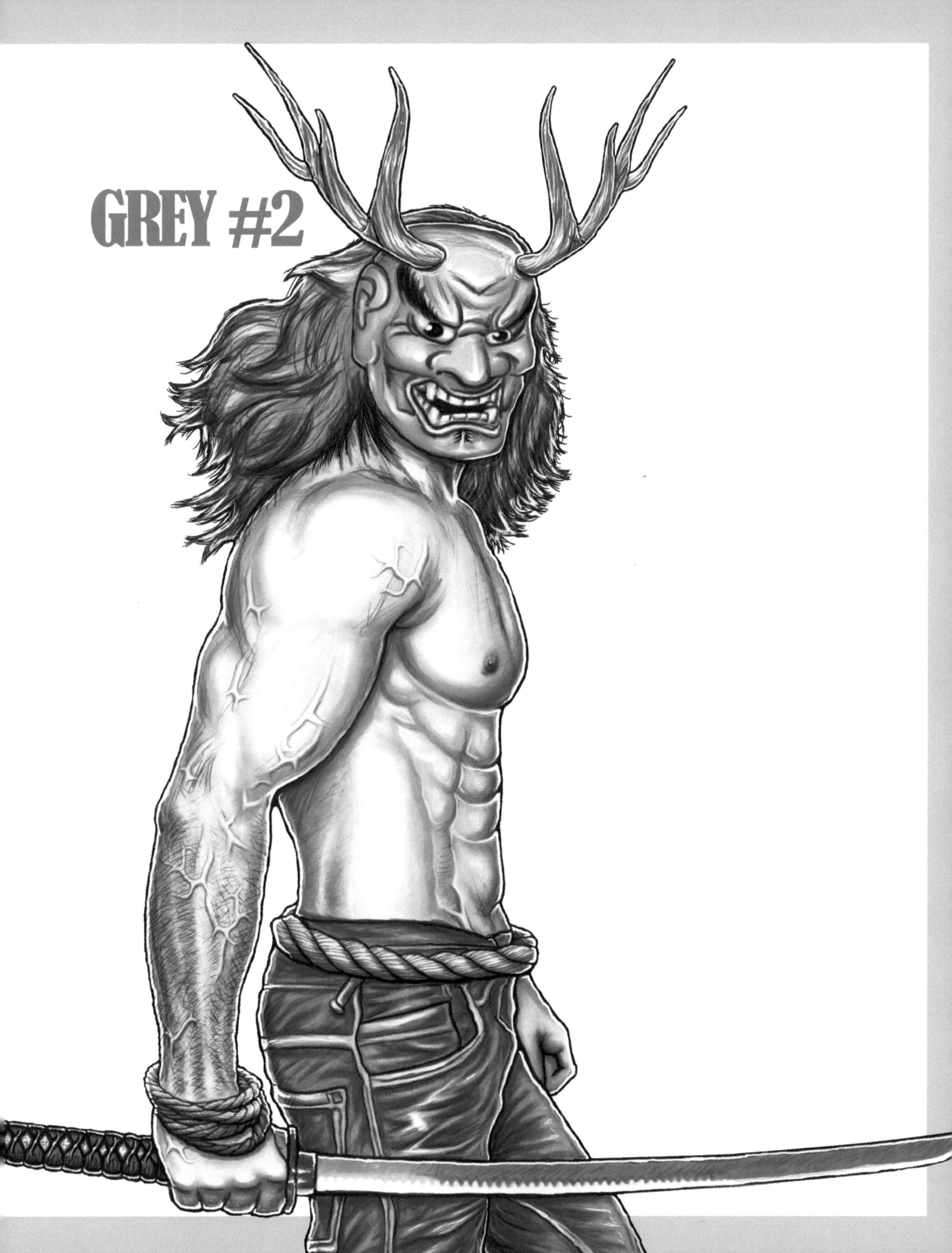

GREY #2

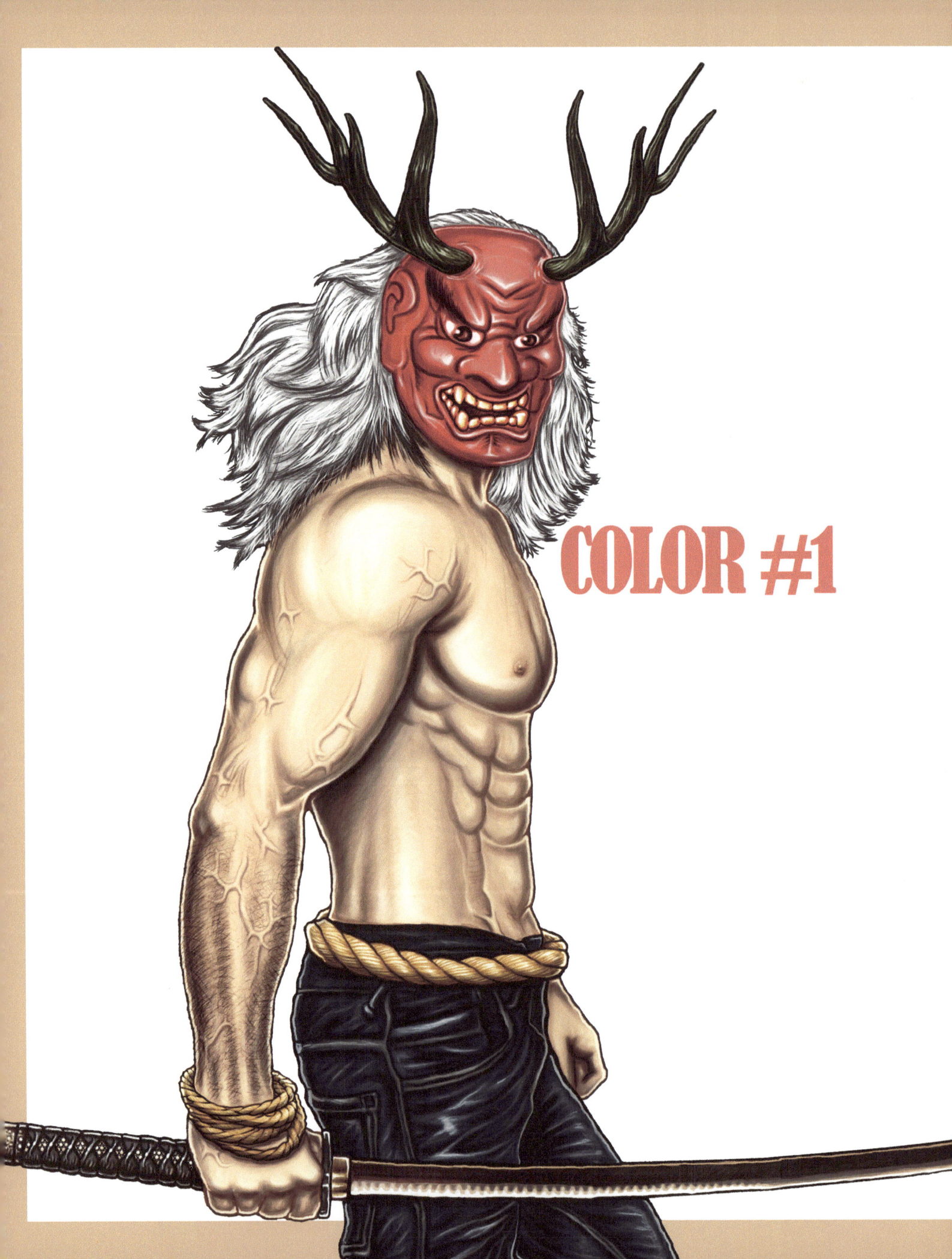

COLOR #1

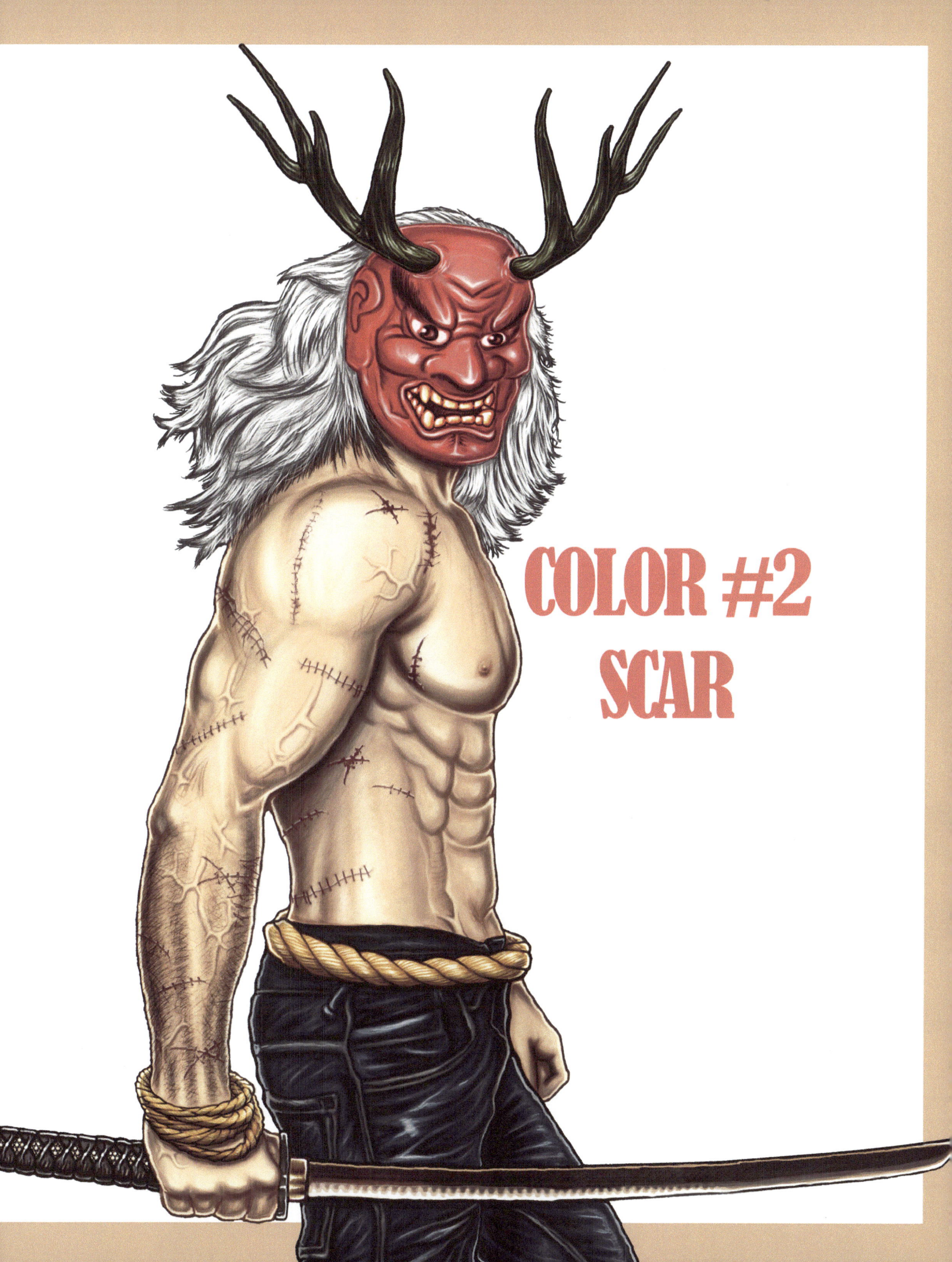

COLOR #2
SCAR

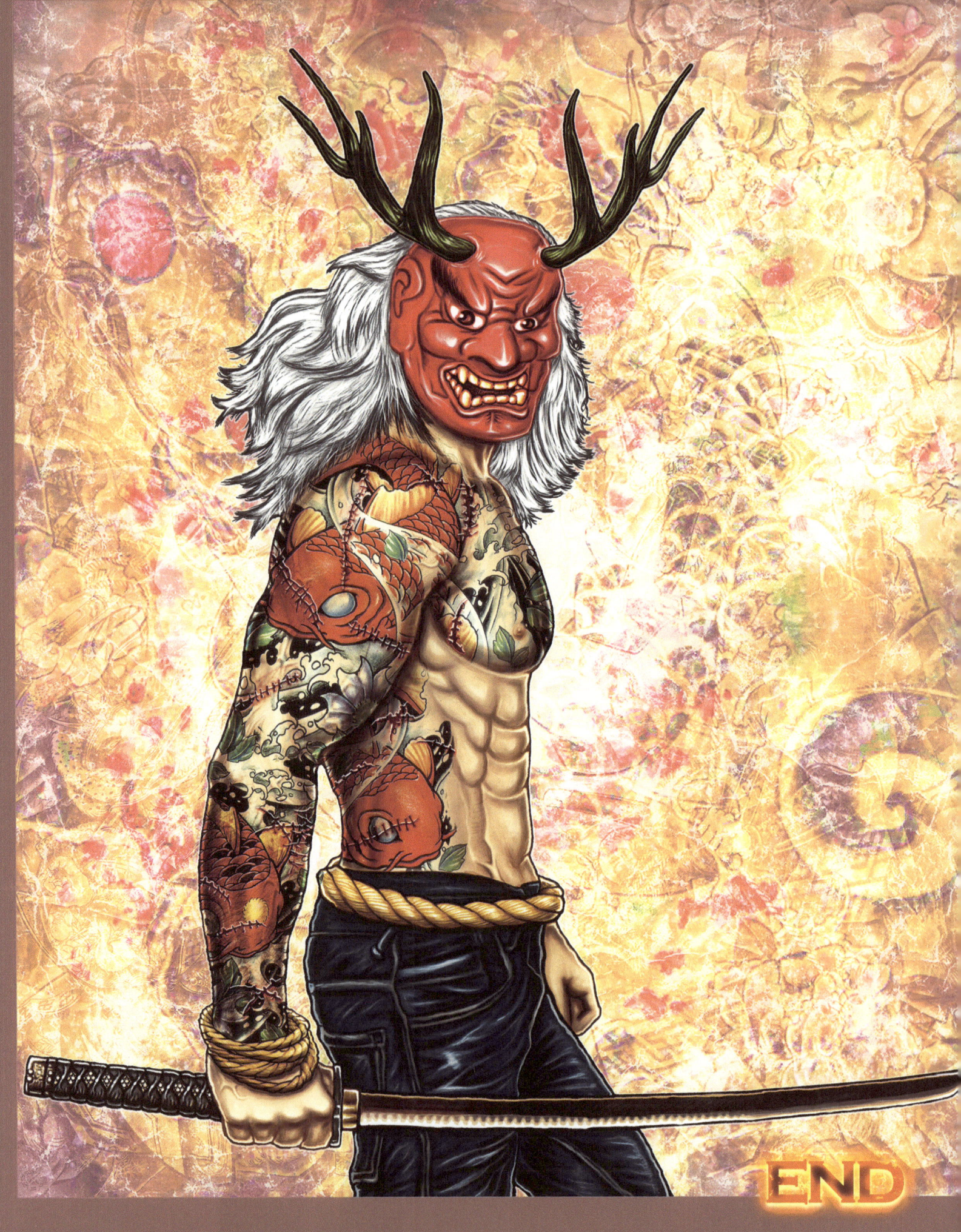

END

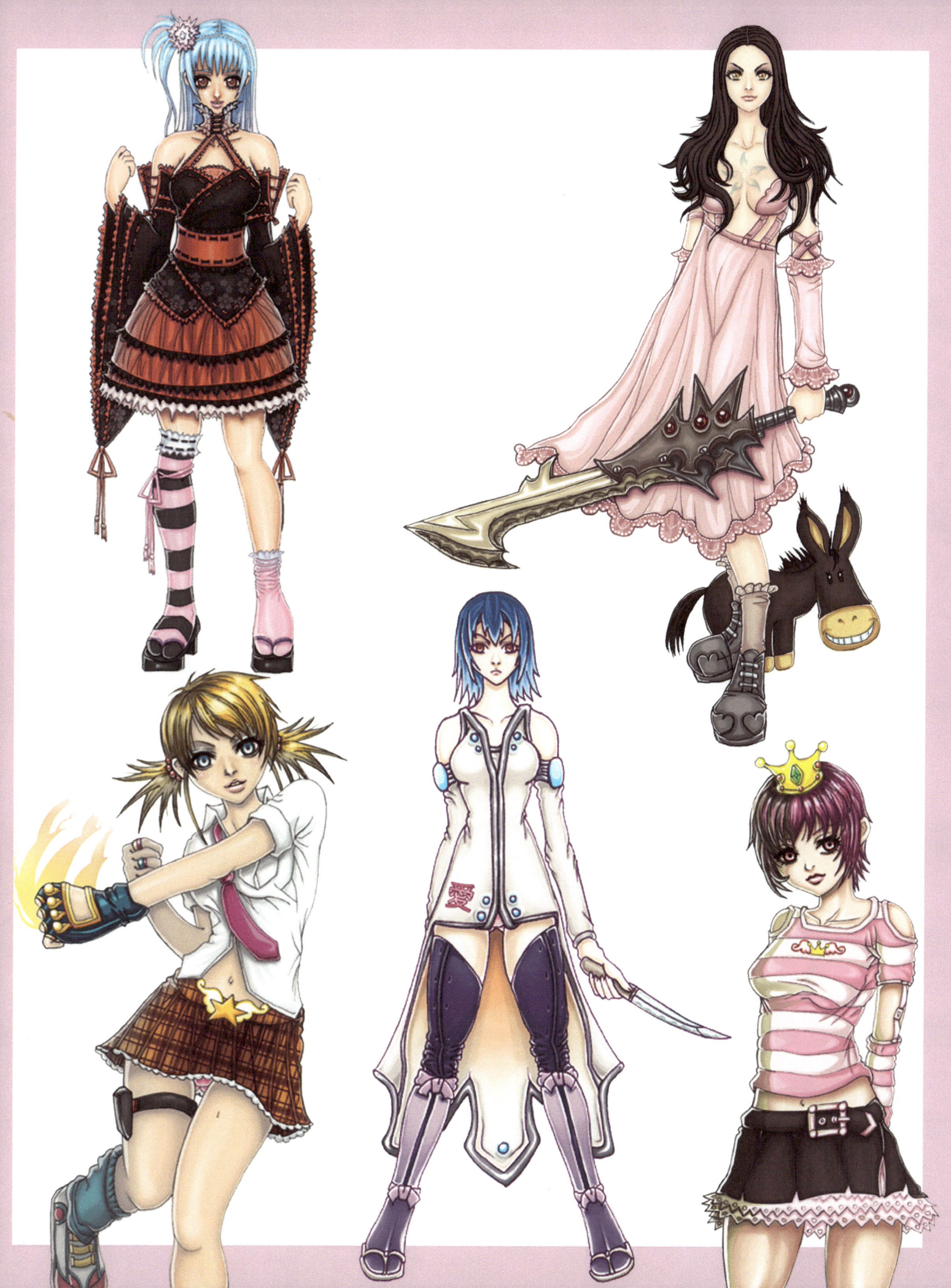

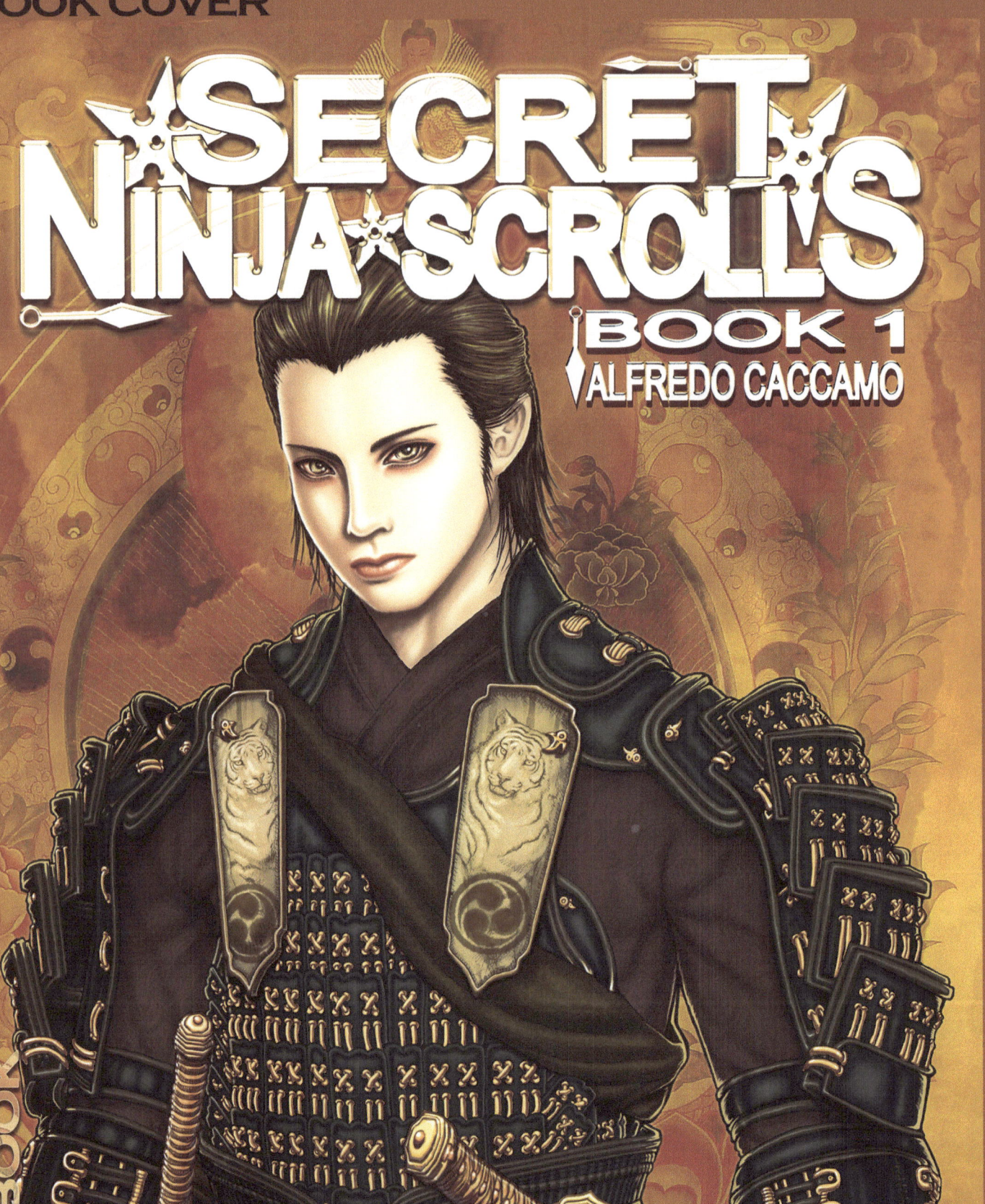

★SECRET★
NINJA★SCROLLS
BOOK 1
ALFREDO CACCAMO

a-BOOK

GOLD EDITION of I ROTOLI SEGRETI DEI NINJA #1

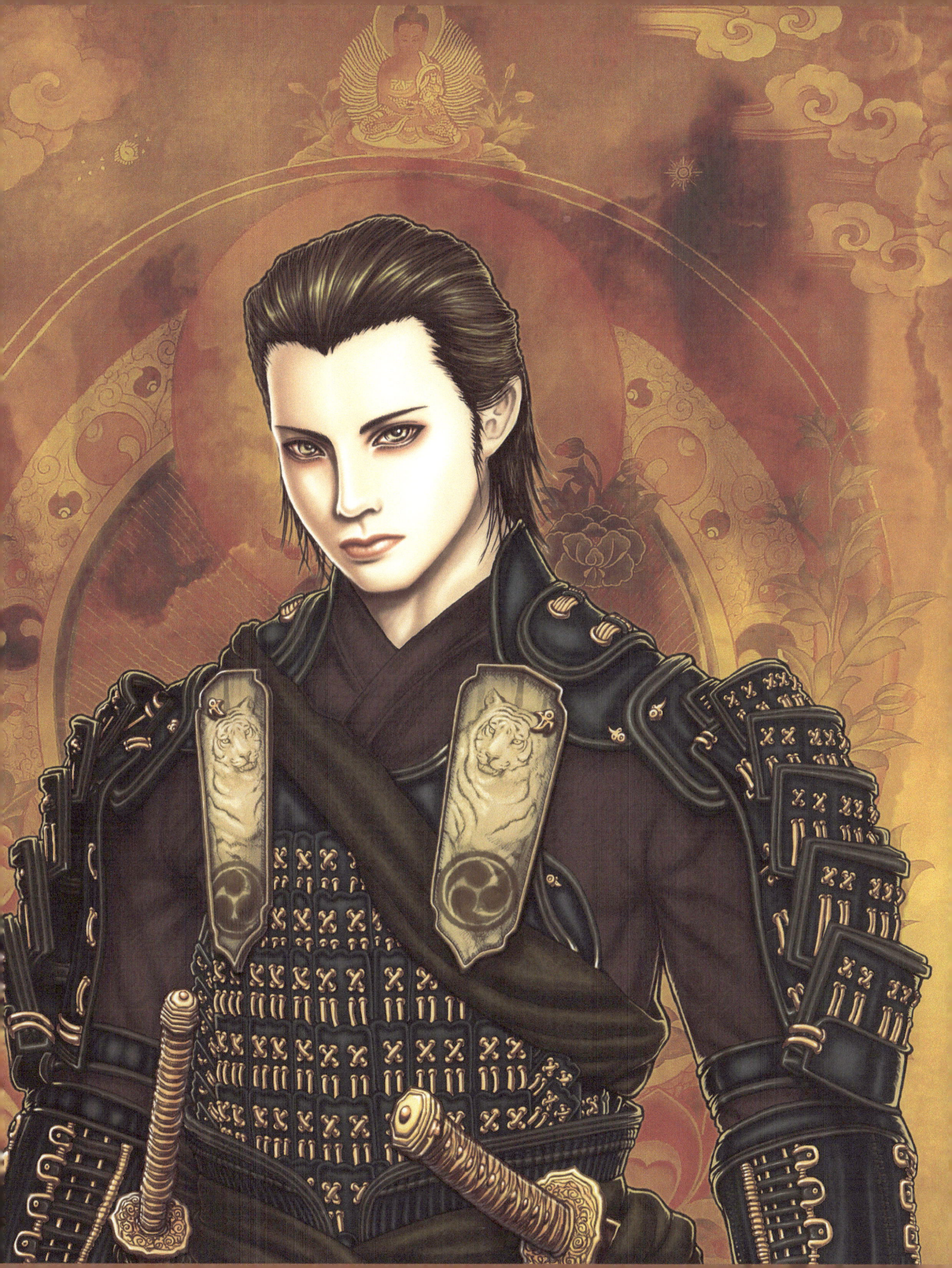

I Rotoli Segreti dei Ninja

Alfredo Caccamo

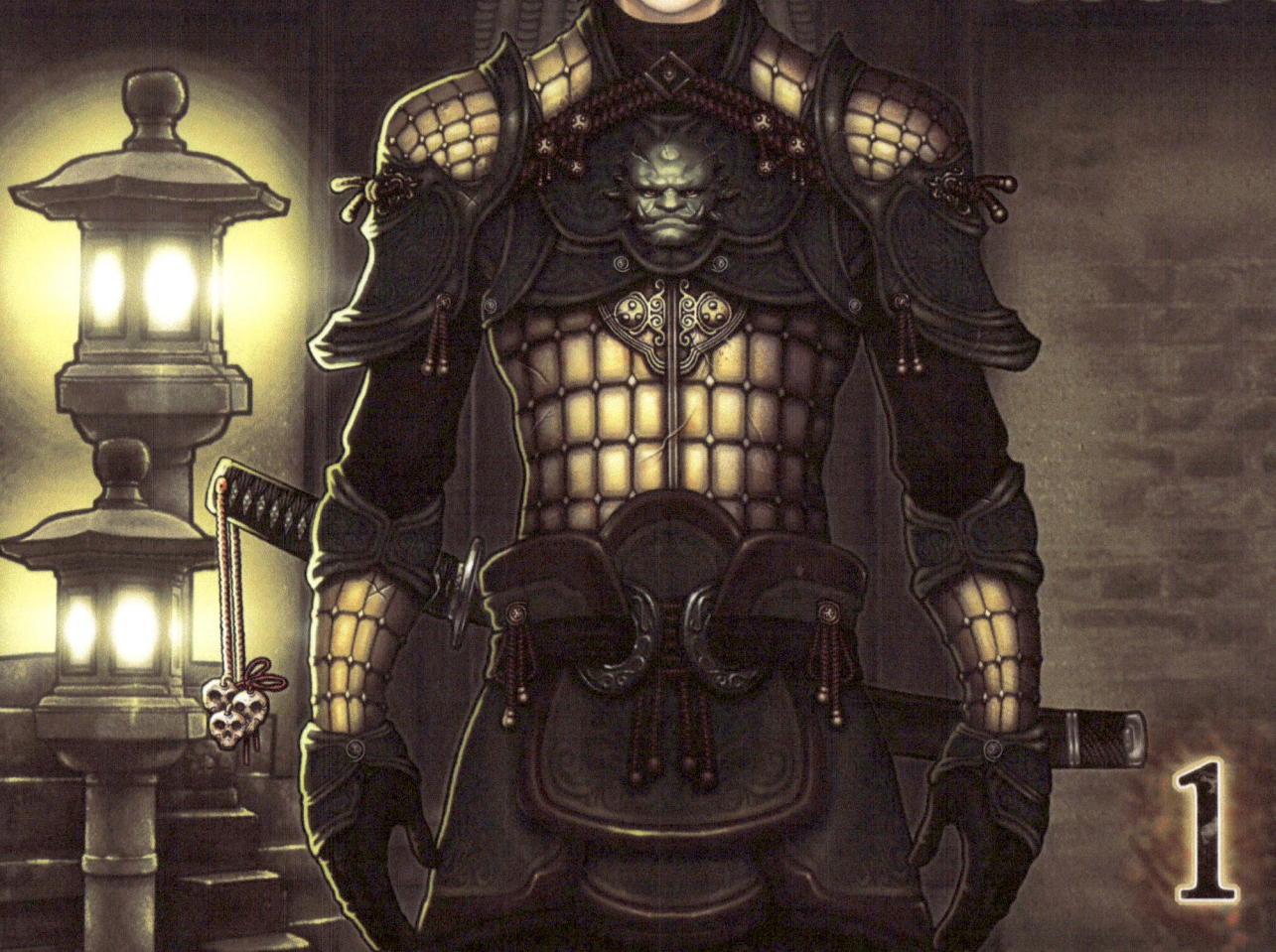

1

REGULAR EDITION OF I ROTOLI SEGRETI DEI NINJA

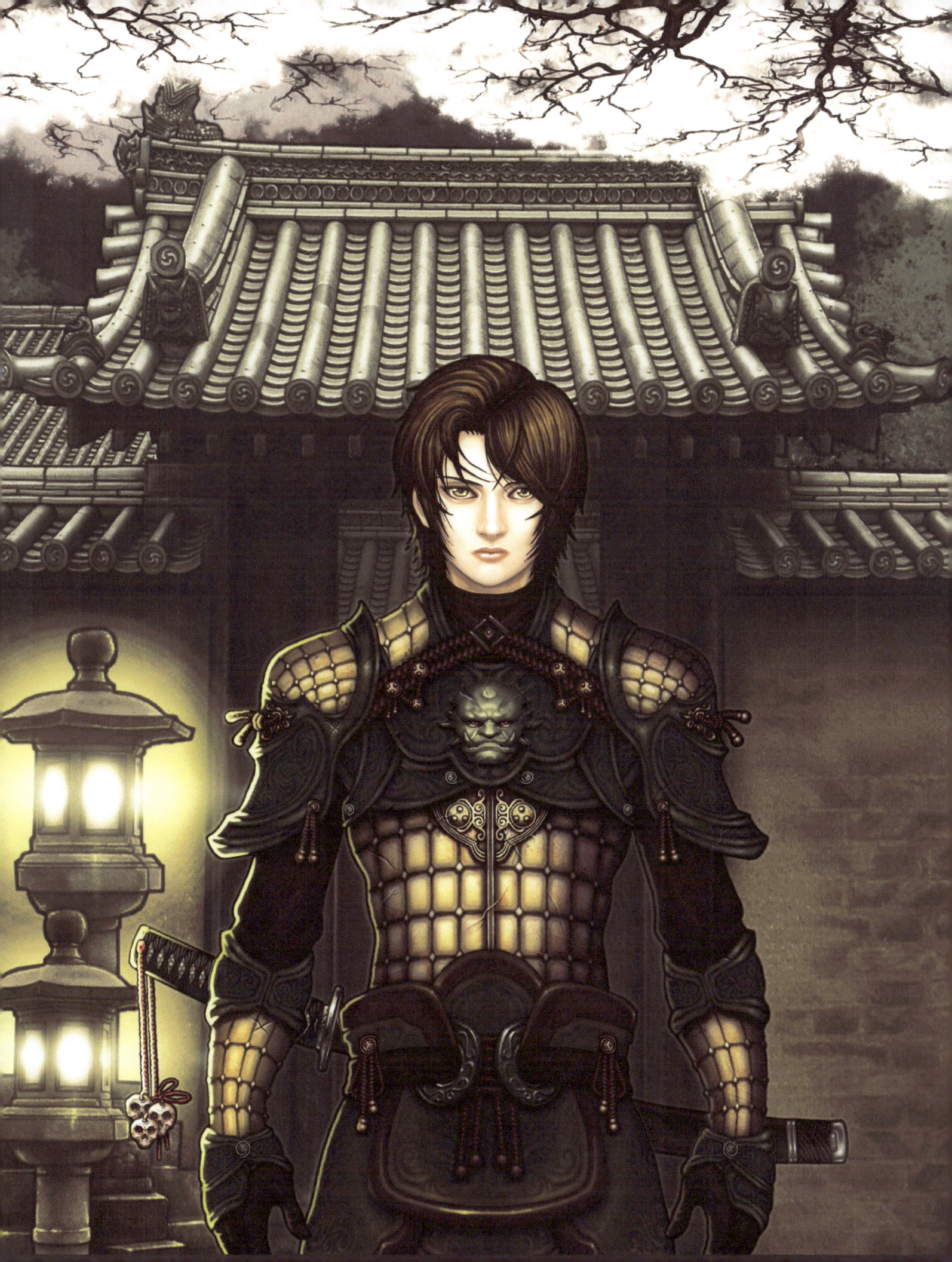

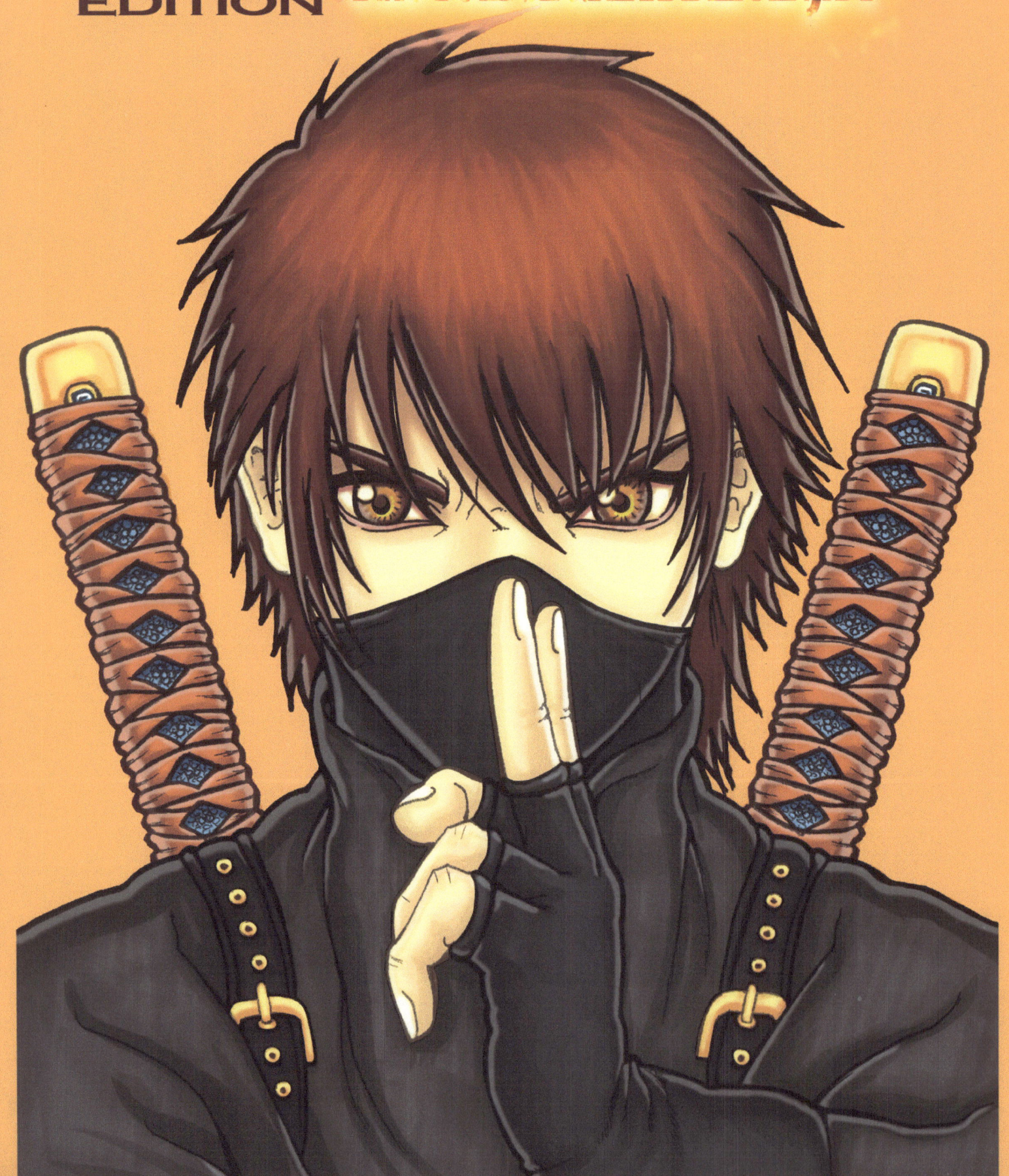

BOOK COVER
VARIANT
EDITION : I ROTOLI SEGRETI DEI NINJA 1

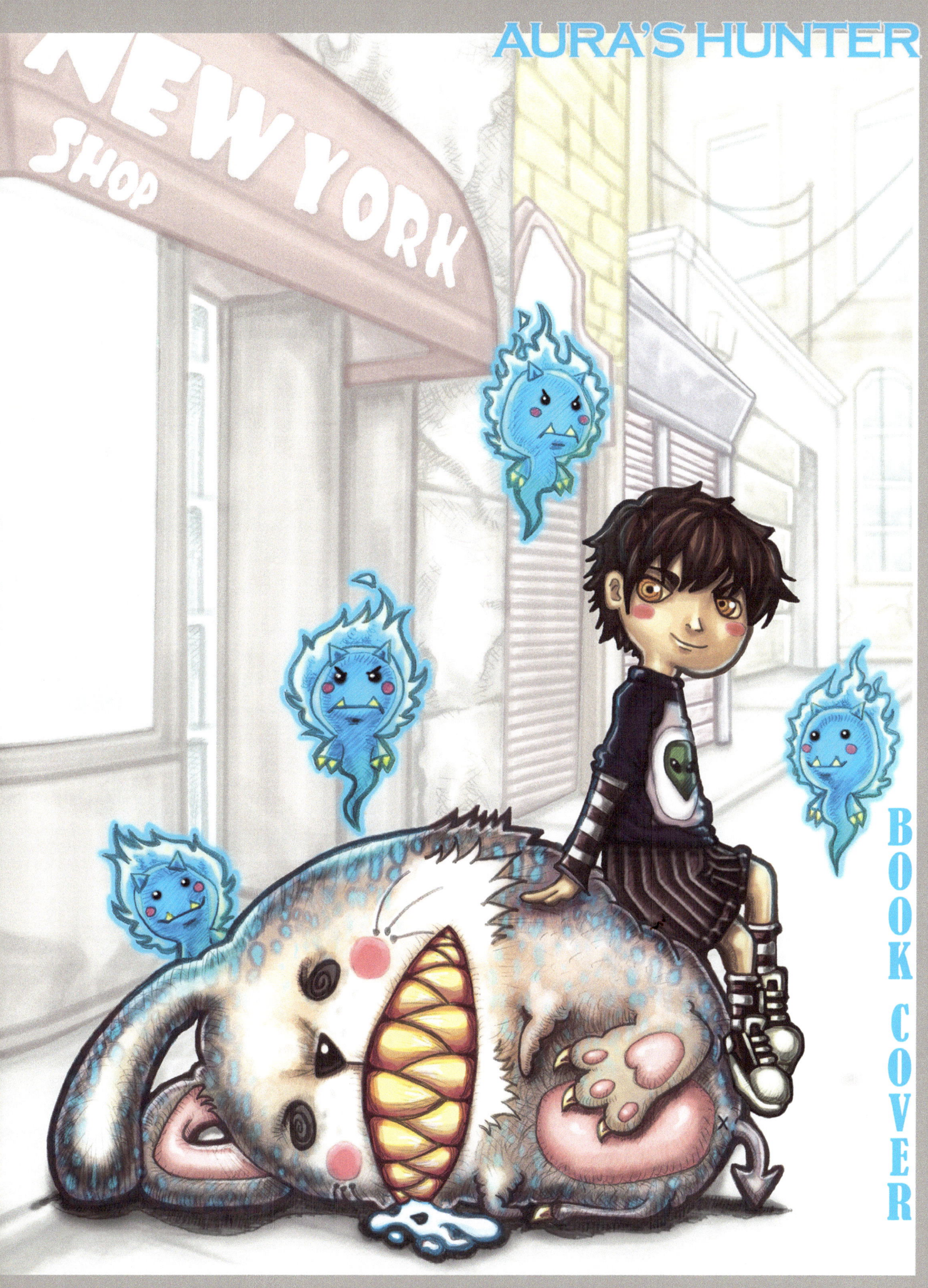

BOOK COVER

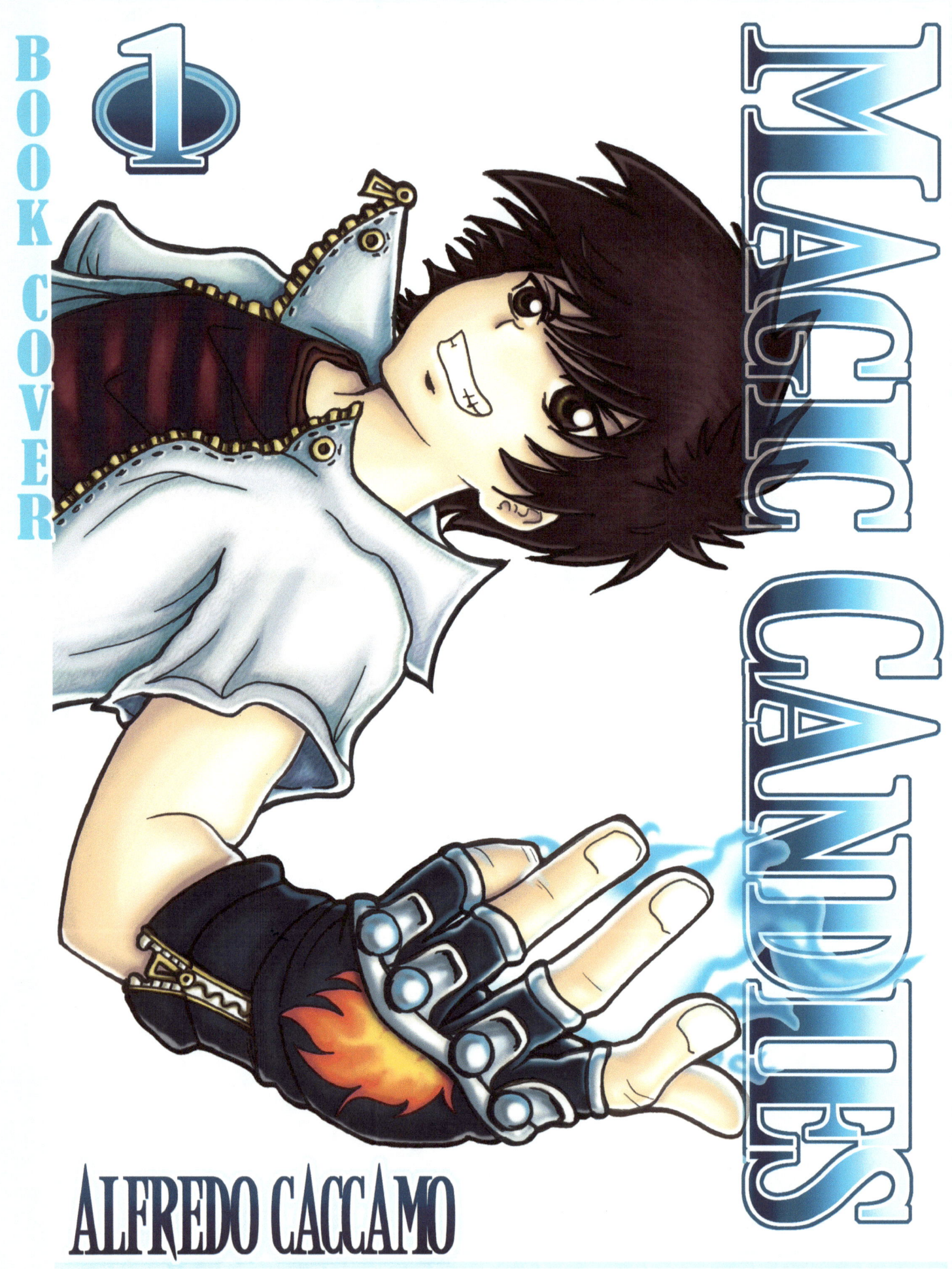

BOOK COVER

1

MAGIC CANDIES

ALFREDO CACCAMO

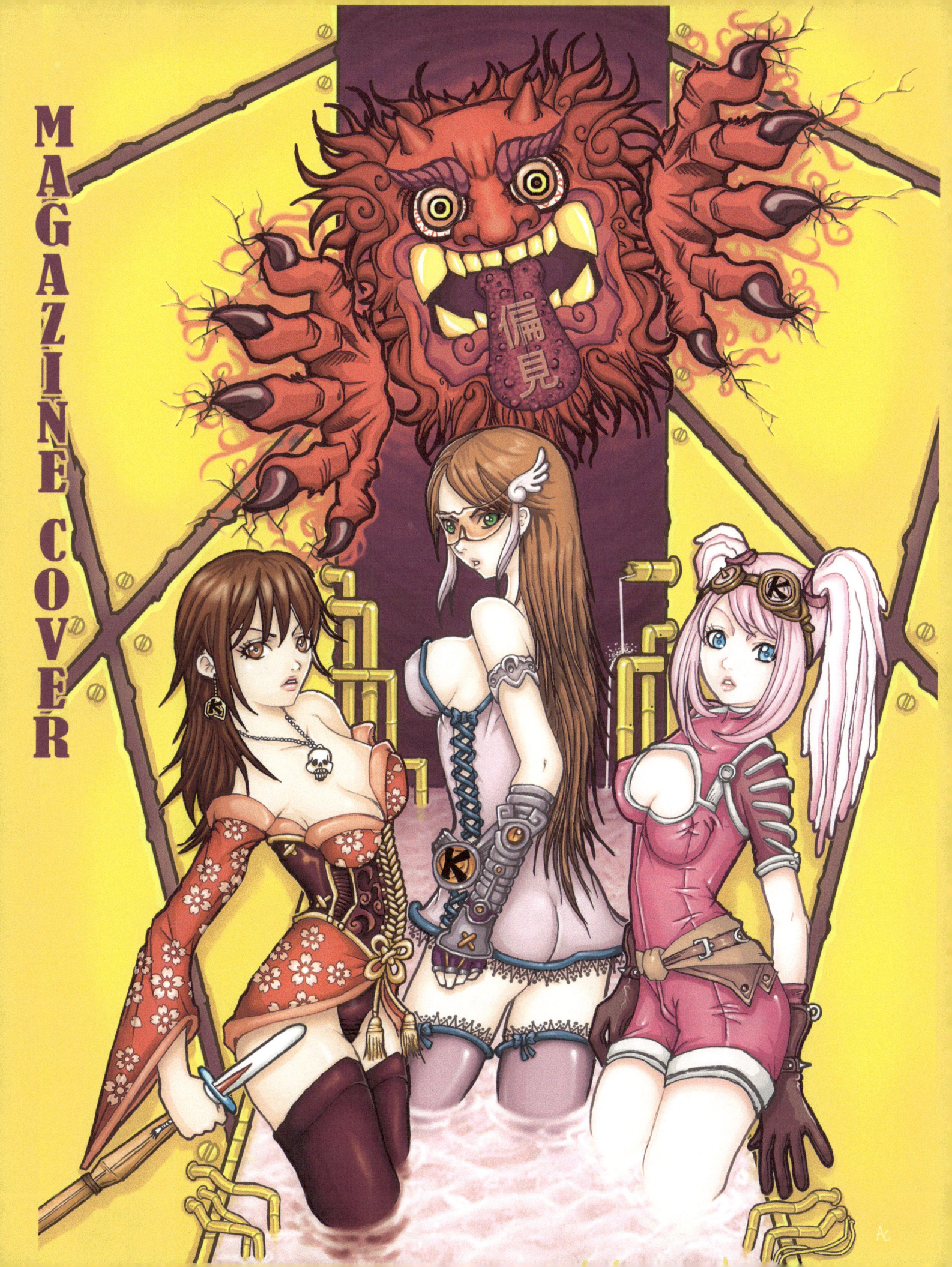

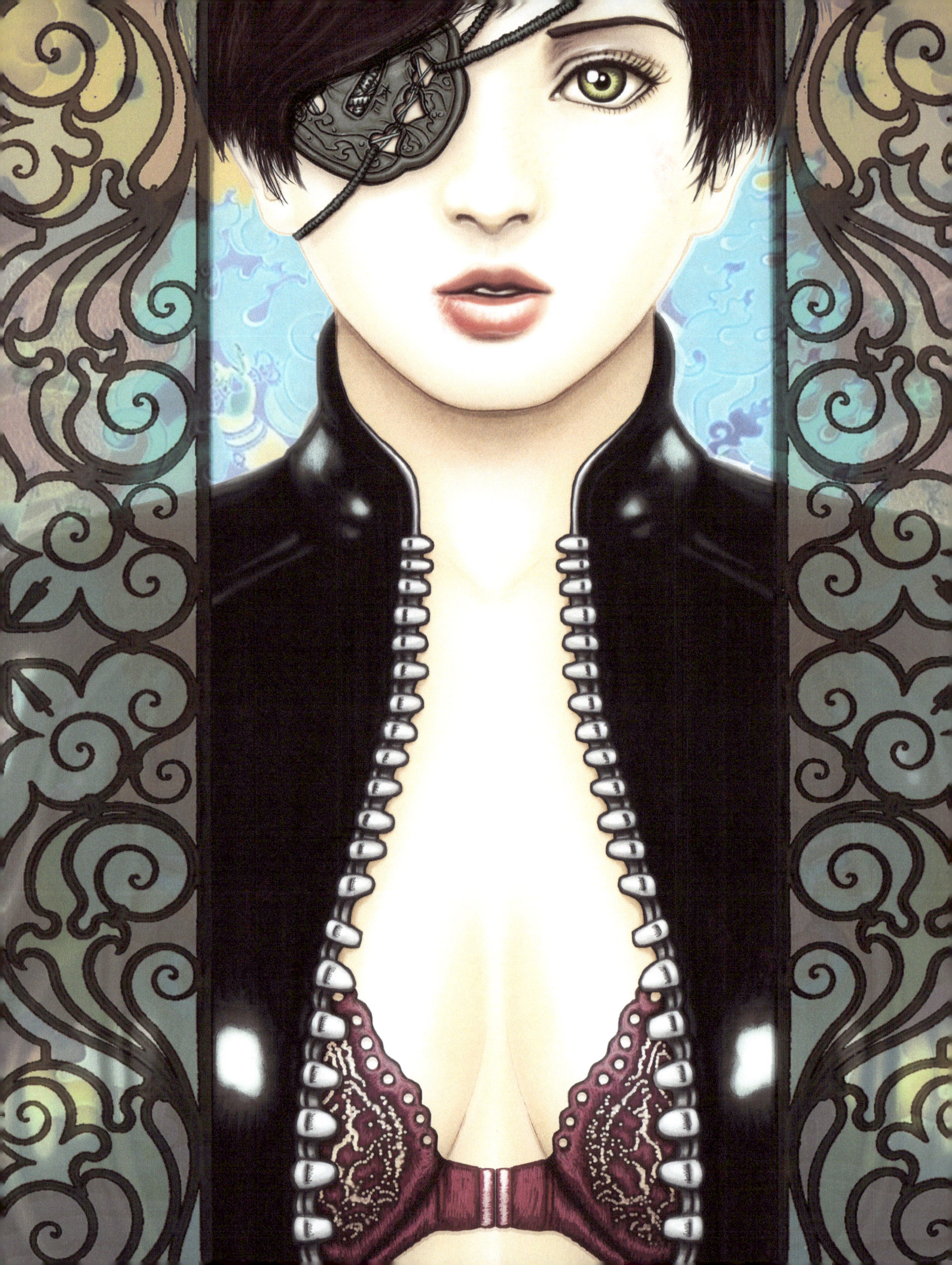

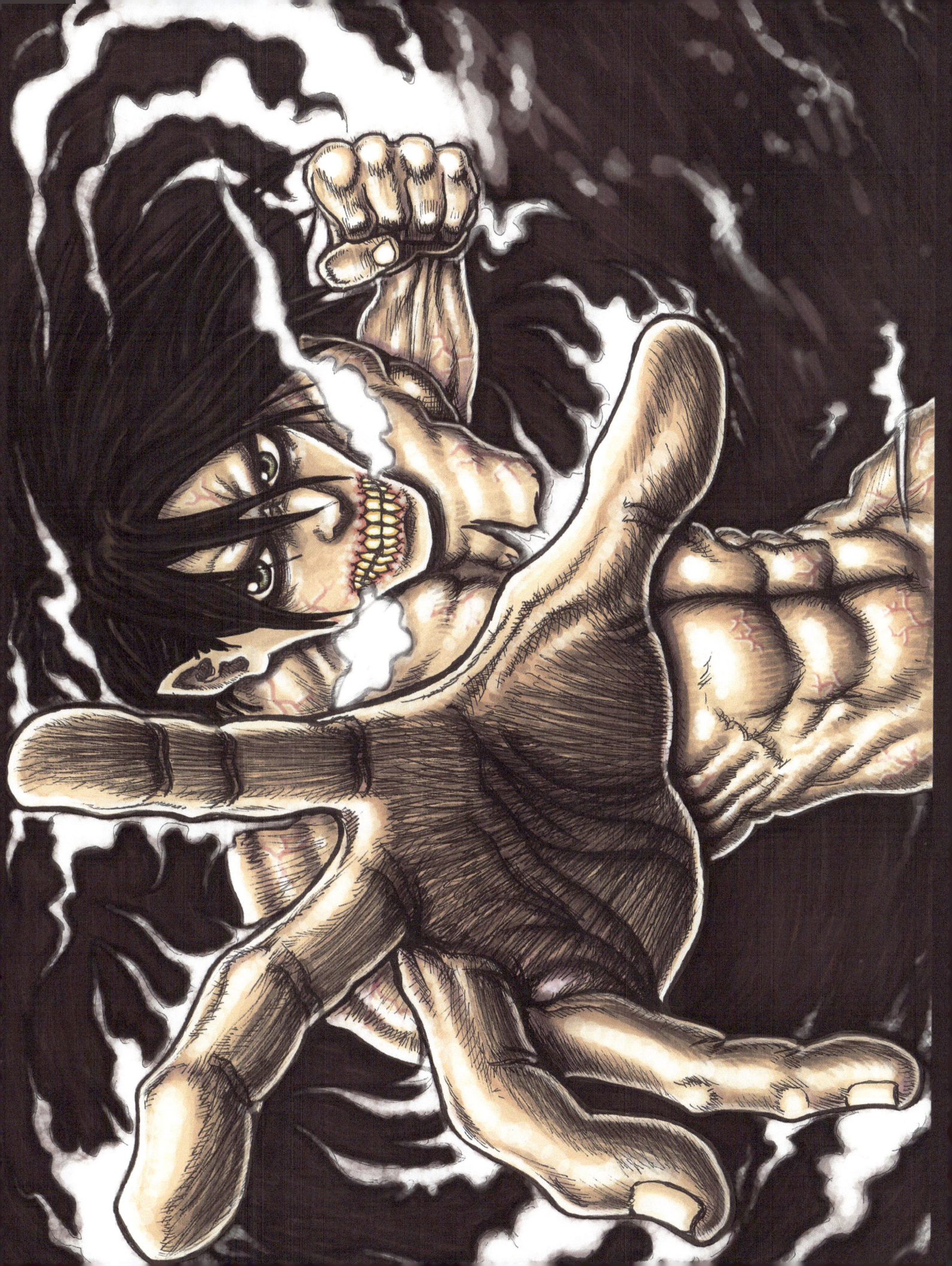

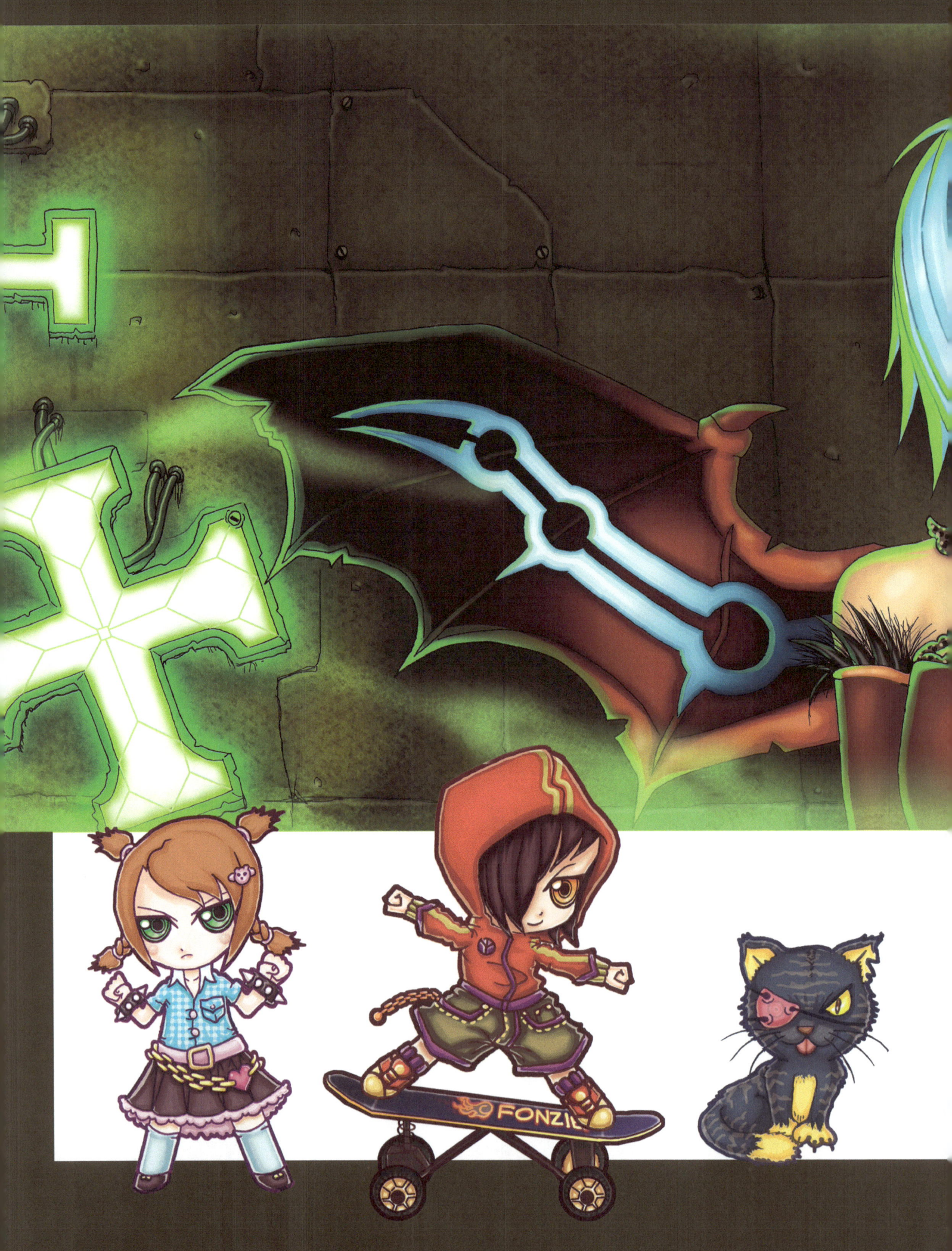

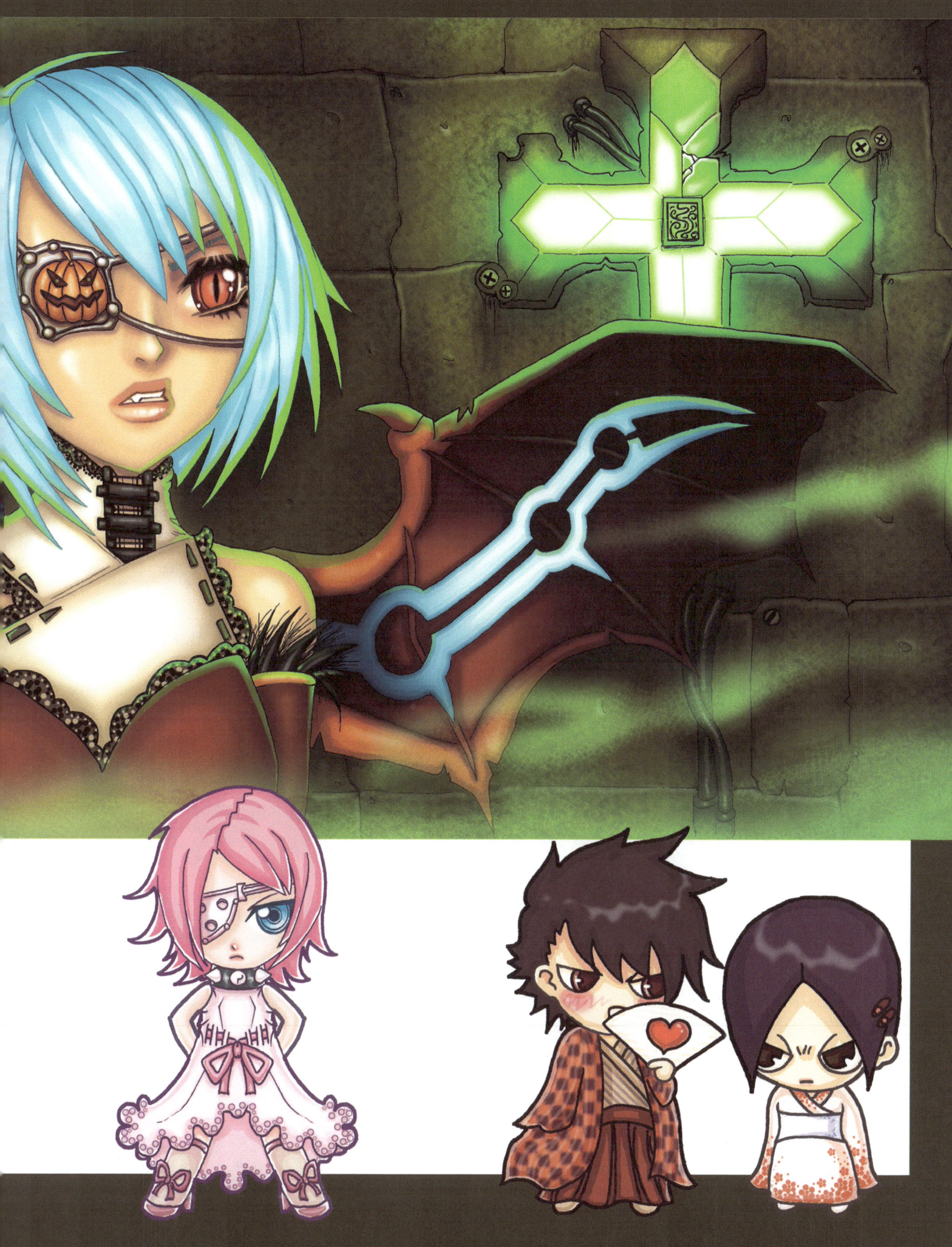

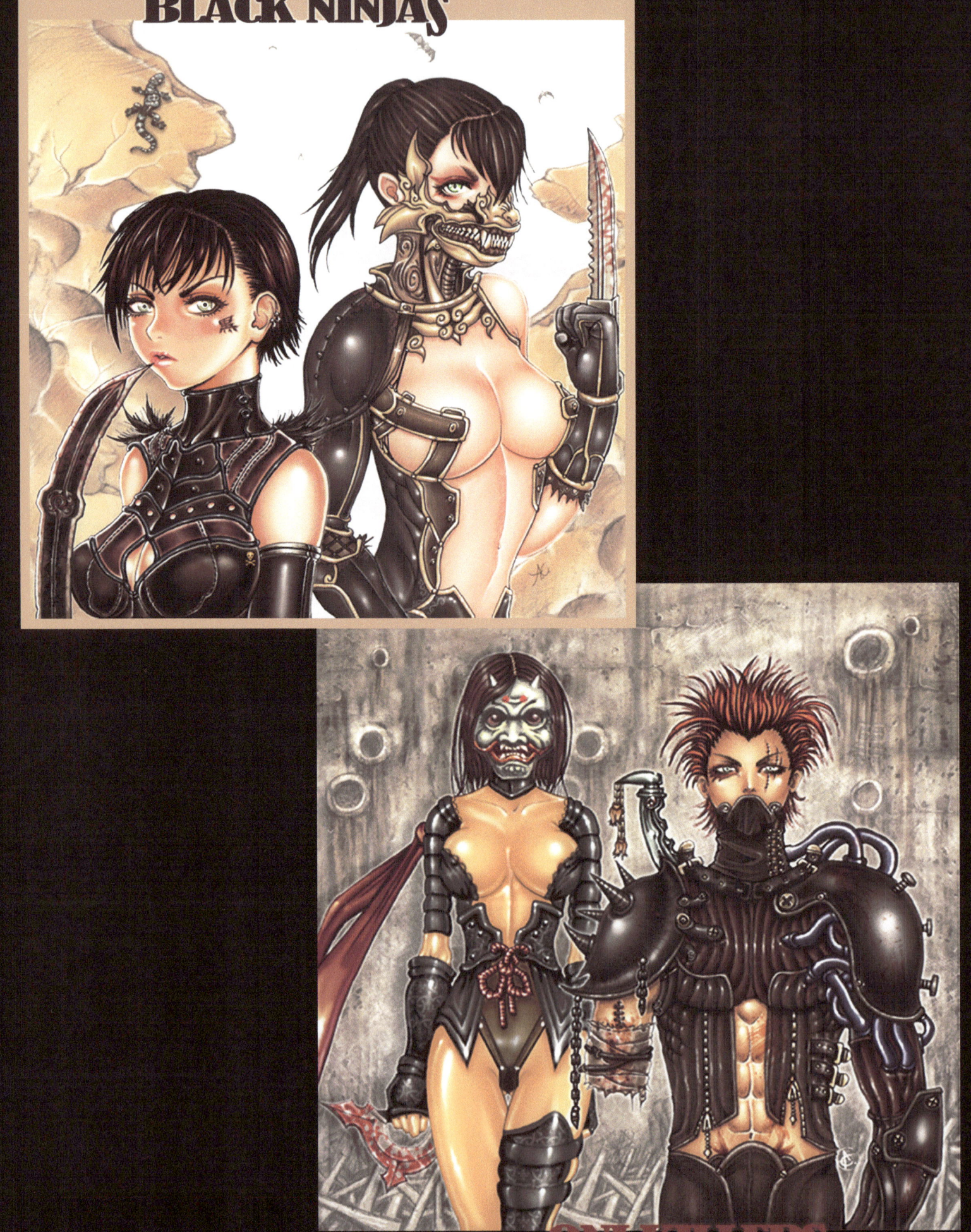

BLACK NINJAS

ONI KILLERS

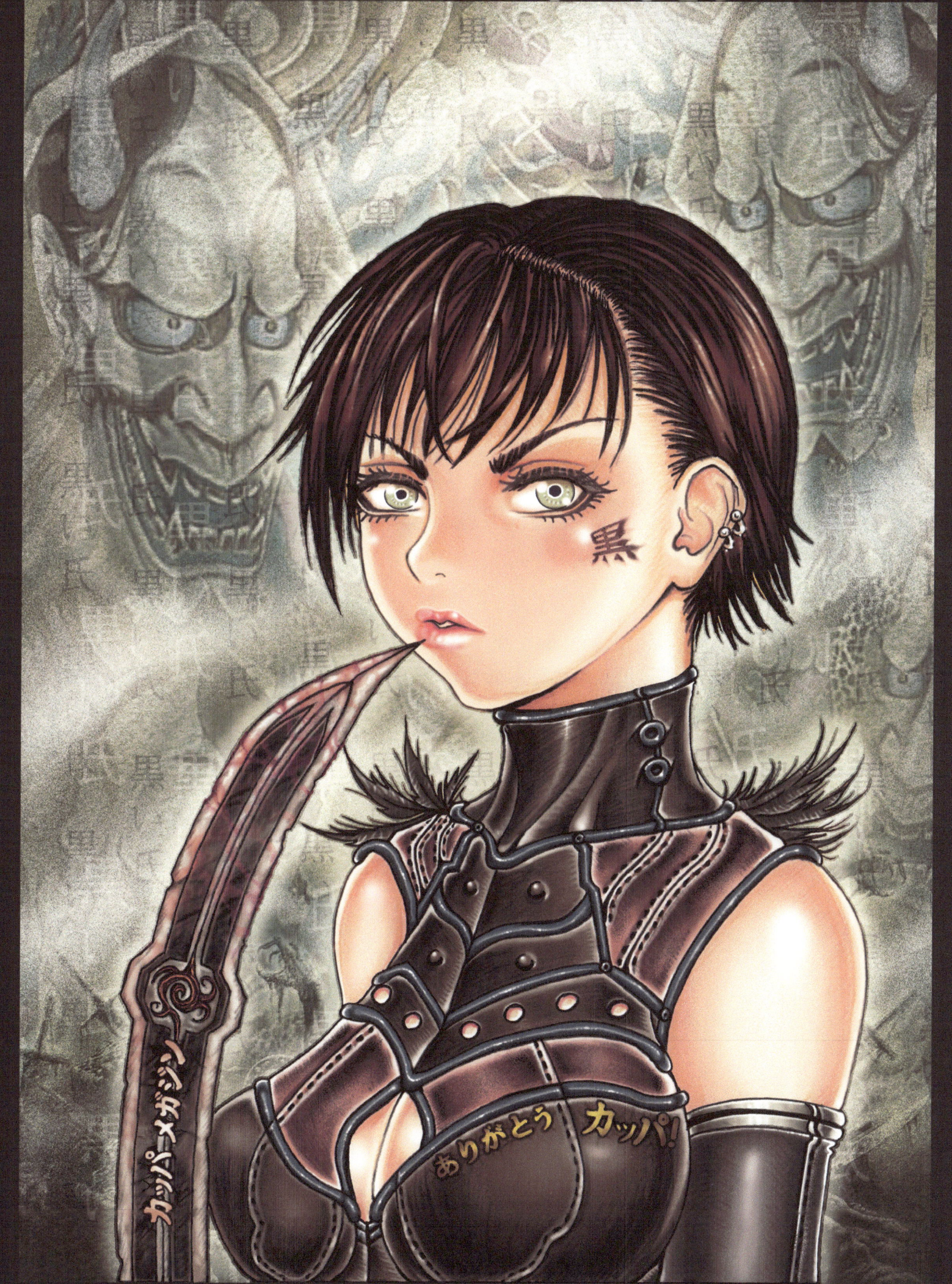

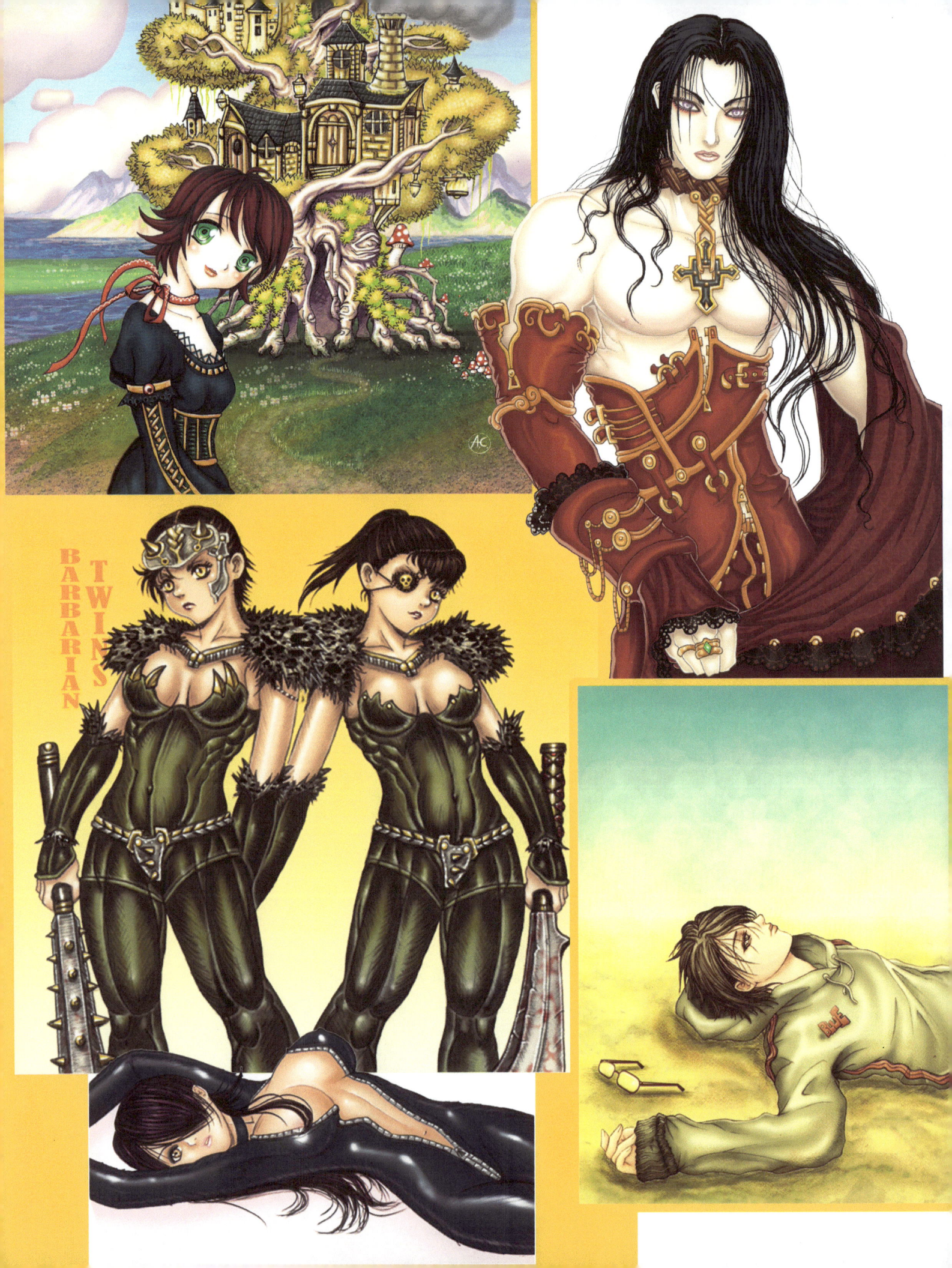

BARBARIAN TWINS

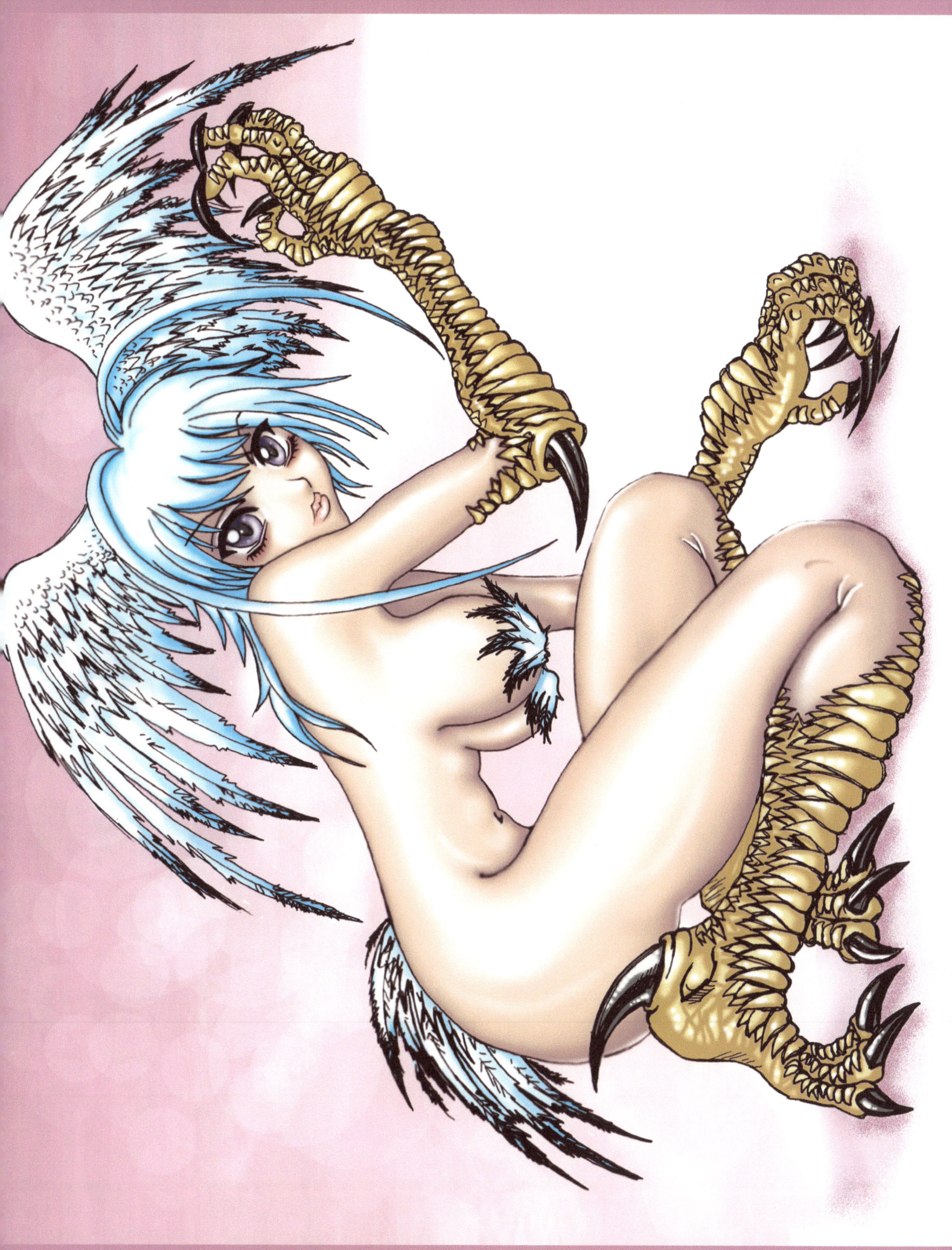

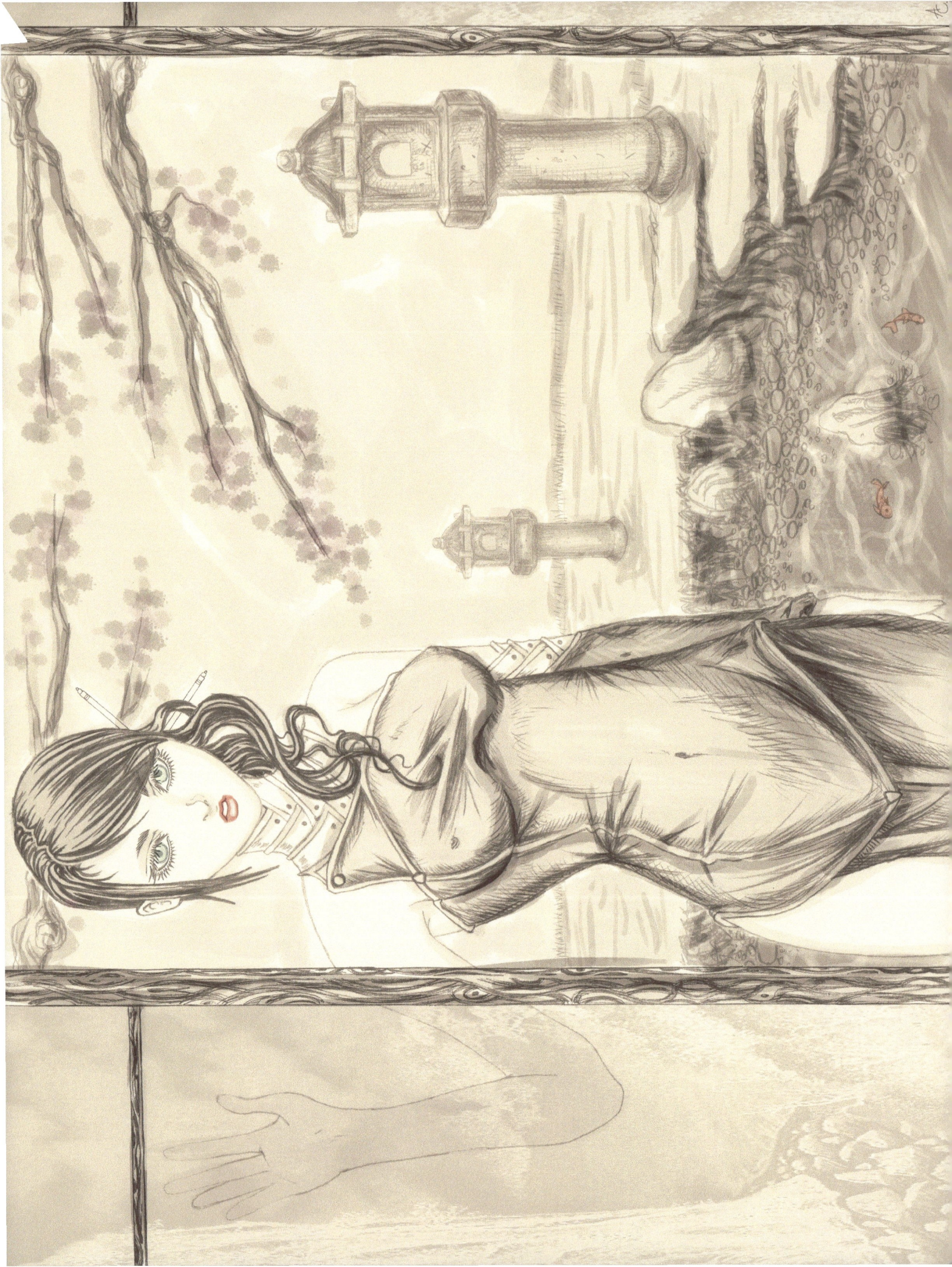